The Let Them Theory

An Innovative Tool That People Everywhere Are Raving About

Sheldon Dashner

© 2025 Sheldon Dashner. All rights reserved.

Please note that unauthorized reproduction, storage, retrieval, transmission, or distribution of this publication is strictly prohibited without the publisher's prior written consent, as outlined in the 1976 US Copyright Act, Sections 107 and 108.

Limitation of Liability/Disclaimer of Warranty:

The publisher and the author provide no guarantees regarding the accuracy or completeness of the contents of this work. They specifically disclaim all warranties, including those related to fitness for a specific purpose. There are no warranties that can be created or extended through sales or promotional materials. Please note that the advice and strategies provided may not be suitable for all situations. This work is sold with the understanding that the publisher is not providing medical, legal, or other professional advice or services. If you need professional assistance, it is advisable to seek the services of a competent professional person. The publisher and author are not responsible for any damages that may occur. Please note that the inclusion of an individual, organization, or website as a citation or potential source of further information in this work does not imply endorsement by the author or publisher. The information or recommendations provided by these sources are not necessarily endorsed. Additionally, it is important for readers to note that any websites mentioned in this work may have undergone changes or become unavailable since the time of writing.

ISBN: 978-1-300-69045-0

Author: Sheldon Dashner

Book Title: The Let Them Theory: An Innovative Tool That People Everywhere Are Raving About

Contents

CHAPTER 1	1
Stop Wasting Your Life on Things You Can't Control	1
CHAPTER 2	11
Start: Allow Them + Allow Me	11
CHAPTER 3	22
Shocker: Life Is Stressful	22
CHAPTER 4	32
Allow Them to Stress You Out	32
CHAPTER 5	40
Allow Others to Form Negative Opinions About You	40
CHAPTER 6	52
How to Love Difficult People	52
CHAPTER 7	62
When Grown-Ups Throw Tantrums	62
CHAPTER 8	71
The Right Decision Often Feels Wrong	71
CHAPTER 9	77
Yes, Life Isn't Fair	77
CHAPTER 10	84
How to Compare with Your Teacher	84
CONCLUSION	95
Your Let Me Era Is Here	95

CHAPTER I

Stop Wasting Your Life on Things You Can't Control

If you struggle to change your life, achieve your goals, or feel happier, listen to this: The problem isn't you. The problem is the power you unknowingly grant to others.

Everyone does it, often without realizing it. You assume that saying the right thing will satisfy everyone. Bend over backward, and your partner might not feel disappointed. Be friendly, and your co-workers will likely like you more. Keep the peace, and your family might stop judging your choices.

I understand this because I've experienced it firsthand. I spent years trying to be everything for everyone else. I believed that if I did enough, said the right things, and kept everyone happy, I would finally feel good about myself.

What happens instead? You put in the effort, stretch your limits, and minimize yourself, yet someone remains disappointed. Someone continues to criticize.

You feel like no matter how hard you try, it's never enough.

This can change. This book helps you reclaim your power. Stop wasting your time, energy, and happiness by trying to control things beyond your reach—such as other people's opinions, moods, or actions. Instead, focus on the one thing you can control: yourself.

Here's the remarkable thing: When you stop managing everyone else, you realize you have much more power than you thought—you've just been giving it away unknowingly.

I want to share with you the simplest, most life-changing idea I've ever discovered: the Let Them Theory.

What Is the Let Them Theory?

The Let Them Theory emphasizes freedom. Two simple words—Let zthem—will liberate you from the weight of managing others. Stop obsessing over what other people think, say, or do, and you will finally have the energy to focus on your own life. Stop reacting and start living.

Stop driving yourself crazy trying to manage or please other people; learn to let them.

What does this look like? Picture yourself at work, and your colleague is feeling down. Don't let their negativity affect you; simply say, "Let them." Let them stay grumpy. This isn't your problem. Concentrate on your tasks and your emotions.

Your dad makes another comment about your life choices, and it hits you like a brick. Don't let it ruin your day; just say Let Him.

Allow him to hold his opinions. You remain unchanged in who you are, what you've accomplished, and your right to make decisions that bring you happiness.

Other people hold no real power over you unless you give it to them.

This is why this works: Stop trying to control things that aren't yours to control, and you will stop wasting your energy. You take back your time, your peace of mind, and your focus. Your happiness depends on your actions, not on someone else's behavior, opinions, or mood.

It sounds simple—and it truly is. This shift will change everything, trust me. This book, titled Let Them, focuses on YOU—your time and your energy—because these are your most precious resources.

The Let Them Theory teaches that allowing others to live their lives enhances your own life. Let people be who they are, feel what they feel, and think what they think. Your relationships will improve as a result.

Letting adults be adults has transformed my life. It will change yours too. When you stop giving your power to others, you will see how much power you truly have.

The most surprising thing about the Let Them Theory is how I discovered it.

I feel a bit embarrassed sharing this story with you.

I found something that transformed my entire approach to life at a high school prom. I never imagined I would write that sentence.

The Prom That Changed My Life

Proms bring a unique kind of stress that's hard to pinpoint. I went through four of them with our two daughters, so I thought our son Oakley's would be easy. I made a mistake.

Our daughters obsessed over every detail for months: dresses, dates, promposals, hairstyles, spray tans, makeup, corsages, bus rentals, post-prom parties. The proms felt never-ending, and I was so glad when they finally ended.

Our son, however, felt uncertain about whether he and his friends would go. He shared no details or plans with us, despite my prodding. Everyone with a son, a brother, or a boyfriend nods along with me right now.

During the week of the prom, Oakley decided he wanted to go. He scrambled at the last minute for everything—the tuxedo, the specific sneakers he wanted to wear, the logistics. Finding his date, a task our daughters agonized over for months, got pushed to the last 48 hours before the big event.

When prom finally arrived, we had the tux, the tennis shoes, the date, and the location of the pre-prom photos all figured out. We ended up hosting the post-prom party. Phew!

Just as we raced out the door, my husband, Chris, adjusted Oak's bowtie one last time. Kendall, our daughter home from college, looked at her brother and said, "You look SO good, Oakley."

I absorbed the moment. He had grown into a handsome young man. I couldn't believe how quickly 18 years flew by. I couldn't believe that Kendall was almost done with college, and our daughter Sawyer had graduated and started working at a large technology firm in Boston.

I stood in the kitchen, feeling the weight of the moment: Time passed, and I wished it would slow down. Time presents a harsh reality. Time will keep moving forward, regardless of your pace. The time you share with the people you love resembles a melting ice cube.

One minute, it exists. . . Next, it disappears.

Here's the sad truth: You and I can't stop the ice cube from melting. We must make the most of the time we have with the people we love while we can. In moments like this, when I really stop and pause, I feel a little sad.

I feel like I race through life and miss the chance to truly enjoy it. I get so worked up about things that don't matter that I ruin the brief moments with those I love.

I stressed out about the last-minute scramble and took it out on Oakley. Absolutely not.

You can probably relate, even if you don't have a child attending the prom.

You might have allowed comments from your family to ruin an entire holiday together, or become so consumed with work or school that you cancel yet another plan with your friends. Years of your life slip away as you get distracted by meaningless things or spend late nights at work. Life can easily overwhelm you, causing you to forget that the main goal is to truly live it.

I stood in the kitchen, watching Chris fix Oakley's bowtie, trying to take it all in. I took a deep breath, walked up to Oak, and hugged him. I gazed at him and said, "You look so handsome."

"Thanks, Mom!" He glanced at the time and exclaimed, "Dude, we gotta go!"

The moment slipped away, and time resumed its march. Life has a funny way of surprising us. You tear up about the passing of time and how old the kids have gotten. Then, you race around trying to find your keys and feel annoyed that someone left their dishes in the sink, AGAIN.

I opened the fridge and grabbed the beautiful corsage I had made from the local flower shop for Oakley's date as I headed out the door. He glanced at it and declared, "Mom, she doesn't want a corsage." "Leave that behind."

He caught my gaze. "It's so beautiful," I said. "Are you certain?"

"I already told you, she said she doesn't want one."

"How about I bring it with us? If she wants to wear it, she can. If she doesn't, that's fine too."

He snapped at me, "Mom, please." "Leave it behind."

I glanced at our daughter Kendall, hoping for some backup. She shook her head at me and said, "Mom, drop it." He feels nervous. He doesn't truly know the girl he asked. "Don't push it."

I felt annoyed and maybe even a little hurt. I spent time scrolling online to research flower trends for prom, ordered his date something really killer, and drove down to get it and pay for it. I tried to do something nice for him, but instead of being grateful, he barked at me. Additionally, it was his first prom—what could he possibly know?

I placed the corsage in my purse and we walked out the door to the spot where everyone was taking pre-prom photos. Upon arrival, Oakley introduced us to his date. She pulled out a boutonniere for his lapel and asked Chris to help her pin it in place. I couldn't help myself.

I reached into my purse, pulled out that corsage like a winning lottery ticket, and said to her: "Oakley said you didn't want something, but I had this made up for you just in case."

Oakley shot me a look, and I instantly regretted speaking up. He faced his date and offered an apology. "Feel free to skip wearing it."

She turned back and said, "It's okay. . . I'll wear it."

I noticed she had made her own corsage and wore it on one of her wrists. Kendall rolled her eyes in exasperation. Chris moved.

I would have evaporated in that moment. Oakley took the plastic container from me and slid the corsage onto the free wrist she had graciously extended. Chris pinned the boutonniere on Oakley's tux.

We snapped a couple of photos, and then, suddenly, rain began to pour. When I say rain, I mean a downpour. The forecast didn't include rain, so none of the 20 kids dressed in black tie, or their parents, wore a rain jacket or carried an umbrella.

I thought these kids will get SOAKED. The kids didn't seem fazed at all. I overheard them in a group discussing, "So, what do you guys want to do for dinner?"

I leaned toward Oakley and whispered, "Oak, don't you guys have a reservation for dinner before the prom?"

No.

I glanced at my husband and exclaimed, "They don't have a reservation for dinner?!"

He shook his head in disbelief. "I suppose not."

My husband and son didn't seem bothered by this. It really bothered me.

How can 20 kids not have any reservations or plans to eat before the prom?

Our daughters managed this months ago.

Oak and his friends discussed their options as a group. I asked them, "So what are you guys going to do for dinner?"

Oakley faced me and said, in that way only a teenage boy can, "I think we're going to head out and go to Amigos."

The Amigos Taqueria stands out as a fantastic taco spot in the heart of town, though it offers only about four tables. The entire place measures the size of a shed.

The moms froze, and the dads began to question the plan.

Twenty kids in black tie planned to head out into the rainstorm without umbrellas or rain jackets to a fast-food joint that maybe ten of them could squeeze inside of. . . before prom?! I couldn't resist.

Do you ever feel like your body races ahead, pushing you to say or do something irrational? I wasn't the only parent who stepped in. Dozens of parents swarmed their kids, trying to take control of the situation. I pulled out my phone and began searching for restaurants with sit-down reservations available for twenty.

Nothing. Nothing existed. Kendall watched me closely. She stood there while I yelled out to the other parents, "I can't find a reservation anywhere." <text"I'll find a pizza place that delivers here."

She reached out, grabbed my arm, pulled me toward her, and looked me in the eyes.

"Mom, if Oakley and his friends want to go to a taco bar for pre-prom, let them."

"But it's too small for all of them to fit in; they're going to get soaked," I stated.

"Mom, LET THEM get soaked!"

"His new sneakers will get ruined."

"ALLOW THEM to get ruined."

"Kendall, you have brand new ones!"

"MOM!" You annoy me. Allow them to arrive at prom in wet tuxedos and dresses. Let them choose where to eat. They have their prom. It doesn't belong to you. "Just let it go."

ALLOW. THEM.

The effect happened immediately. I felt something inside me soften. The tension disappeared, my mind stopped racing, and the stress of trying to control what was happening evaporated. Why did I have to get involved?

Why did I need to handle this situation? Why not focus on what I will do for dinner tonight, instead of what they will? Why did I stress about them at all?

Allow them. The prom belongs to them, not you. Stop controlling, judging, or managing it, and LET THEM.

I did that. I walked up to Oakley and smiled while the other parents tried to micromanage their kids. "What now?" he asked. "I'm giving you forty dollars for Amigos," I said. "Enjoy your prom!"

He smiled broadly, wrapped his arms around me tightly, and said, "Thanks, Mom." We will.

Then I saw Oak and his date step out the door and into the pouring rain. They ran through the storm, splashing mud onto her gown and ruining his new sneakers. I didn't care. It was quite cute.

One moment fundamentally changed my entire approach to life.

Researching the Theory

For the past two years, I have researched the Let Them Theory, exploring why it works and how you can use it to transform your life and enhance your relationships with others.

I spoke to many of the world's leading experts in psychology, neuroscience, behavioral science, relationships, stress, and happiness while writing this book. As you read the book, you will meet them, and their research will help you apply the theory in countless situations in your life. The science is clear: This thing works. It works really well.

This book goes beyond simply introducing you to the Let Them Theory. A fundamental law of human nature exists: Every human being has a hardwired need for control.

Everyone possesses an innate desire to control every aspect of their lives: their time, their thoughts, their actions, their environment, their plans, their future, their decisions, and their surroundings. You feel in control, which brings comfort and safety. As a result, you often try to control everyone and everything around you, sometimes without even realizing it.

However, you cannot control one thing. You can try as hard as you want, but you cannot control or change another person. You control only yourself. Your thoughts drive your actions and shape your feelings.

You have worked against this fundamental law of human nature for too long. You fight to change people, battle to control situations, and worry about what others say, think, or do. In doing so, you create unnecessary stress, tension, and friction for yourself and in your relationships. I also did.

The Let Them Theory has changed my entire approach to life and how I interact with others. I embraced the natural flow of human nature instead of resisting it. I stopped wasting my energy on things I can't control—what others say, think, and do—and focused my energy on what I can control: myself.

The outcome? I have more control over my life than ever before. It freed me. I took responsibility for my actions, and as a result, my relationships improved in ways I never thought possible. Unlocking a door that had been sealed shut for years felt exhilarating. What lies behind it? A life where I embrace freedom from the burden of managing others.

In the coming pages, you will discover the theory, find the easiest way to start using it, and experience how awesome it feels when you do. Discover a surprising finding I made early in our research. The Let Them Theory goes beyond simply letting them. Yes, it starts with these two words, but that's just part of the story. Let Them serves as only the initial part of the equation. A second, even more crucial step to this theory is to let me.

In the next chapter, we will unpack both Let Them and Let Me and explore the science and psychology behind each of the two steps. You will learn about the eight core areas of your life where the theory will create the biggest positive impact. Let's discuss your relationships, career, emotions, opinions, stress, love life, struggles, chronic comparison, friendship, and most importantly, your relationship with yourself.

You will repeatedly discover that you have been trying to control the wrong things and have unknowingly turned other people into a problem. Other people should serve as one of the greatest sources of happiness, support, and love in your life. They cannot be if you continue to control what they feel, say, and do. This book concludes here.

Master the Let Them Theory, and you will stop exhausting yourself by trying to control the uncontrollable. This goes beyond simply feeling better. Redesign your entire life. I'm excited for you to explore the space and freedom to live your life as you've always desired—on your terms.

Let's get started.

CHAPTER 2

Start: Allow Them + Allow Me

Shortly after I discovered the Let Them Theory, I sat on my couch, scrolled through social media, and spotted a photo of an old friend. She looked amazing. I looked down to read the caption, where she described an amazing weekend she just had with her friends. She meant it, and I could tell.

I admired how tan, happy, relaxed, and refreshed she looked as I stared at the photo. I thought, Wow. I really want a weekend like that. I could really use a spray tan. I swiped through the carousel of photos and saw one epic girls' weekend after another.

Enjoy brunch. Dance. Shop. Joyful sounds fill the air. Swim. Cocktails are delightful.

I pinched with my thumb and pointer finger to zoom in for a closer look at the group shot, and I realized I knew every single one of the women smiling back at me on my screen. I felt my heart sink. All my friends went away together.

You feel that awful sensation in your stomach when you realize you've been left out. It feels like a punch. You brush it off, telling yourself it's not a big deal, but the hurt feels real. I could have put my phone down, but I chose not to.

I scanned those photos one by one, witnessing a girls' trip through the eyes of the same women with whom I had raised my kids in our small suburban town. I made an effort not to let it bother me. It happened.

Details began to fill my mind. I pictured the fun they had and the closeness they achieved. I knew these women for years. We bonded through barbecues, carpools, soccer games, date nights with our spouses, and tough conversations about parenthood. I began to spiral.

I'm speaking: Completely. Someone who stalks. Mode. I sat on that same spot on the couch, feeling it mold to my back as I poured over each of their accounts. Five minutes ago, I felt perfectly fine. What about now? I felt the familiar swirl of emotions take over: rejection, insecurity, confusion. When did they schedule this? Why did they not include me? Why do I never receive invitations anywhere? When did I last go away with friends?

While I scrolled through their photos, turning those questions over in my head, Chris walked into the room, glanced at me, and asked, "What's wrong?"

I sighed and told him the truth: "I just found out that a bunch of my girlfriends went away for the weekend on a really fun trip." I clearly didn't receive an invitation.

"That sucks," he exclaimed.

"I might have done something wrong," I said. "They might be mad at me."

He crossed his arms and asked, "Why do you care so much?"

He caught my gaze.

"You're not really close friends with them anymore, Mel."

He is right. I knew he was there. I still felt the urge to reach out and smooth things over. You've likely experienced this before. You discover that you weren't included in something, and you seek reassurance that you didn't do anything wrong.

I honestly didn't know. If you're anything like me, you immediately assume you've done something wrong when it happens. I sat on the couch, searching my mind for any evidence of why I wasn't included, but nothing came to me. That increased my nerves.

We had known each other for years. We experienced early motherhood together, we shared many life moments, and I truly liked everyone on that trip. I hadn't spent time with them as a group in a long time. I saw them around town at large gatherings, but I didn't invest in those individual friendships. I also didn't plan anything fun or reach out to them recently. I understood this intellectually, but emotionally, I felt devastated. I felt like I returned to middle school: the one left out of the sleepover, the one who didn't make the team, or the one who wasn't part of the inside joke.

Putting the Theory into Practice

I wanted to reach out to them and fix it. Reach out, message. I need something to make the anxiety disappear. Those two words came in and saved me from myself. Allow them.

I used to obsess over this for days. It's been weeks, truly. I let my emotions get the best of me. I tried to pretend it didn't bother me. I tried to convince myself that I didn't care. I tried to rationalize it over and over in my mind. I turned my friends into villains to feel better. All of this made me feel worse and pushed me to withdraw even more from these women I genuinely liked.

However, that did not occur. I felt bothered for about 10 minutes. I felt a little better as soon as I said Let Them. Saying it a second time made me feel a little better. The third, fourth, fifth, sixteenth, and thirtieth times I said it, I felt a little better.

I will be honest with you: In these painful situations, you must keep saying Let Them over and over, because when something hurts, the hurt doesn't just disappear. It keeps rising again and again. Don't be surprised when you find yourself repeating Let Them over and over.

Allow them to go on the trip. Allow them to spend the weekend together. Allow them to enjoy themselves without your presence.

Initially, those words struck me as a rejection. I felt like I was surrendering. But then I realized something important: Let Them focused on standing firm. I aimed to free myself from the control I never possessed in the first place. The truth is that no matter how much I analyzed the situation or how many ways I tried to control or fix it, nothing I did changed what had happened. Their decision to leave shouldn't have made me feel bad, but my efforts to control the situation left me feeling horrible.

Allow them.

The knot in my chest began to loosen. The pressure to "fix" the situation faded, and I realized something that changed everything: Their weekend away had nothing to do with me.

They didn't take it personally. They did not plot against me. They did not make a statement about my worth. What if they were? Allow them.

What We're Really Trying to Control

Everyone experiences moments when they attempt to control their surroundings—especially during times of hurt, exclusion, annoyance, or fear. You might find yourself managing every detail of a group plan to ensure everyone is included, or stressing over whether people are upset with you when they don't respond to your messages promptly. Isn't it exhausting?

I naturally take on the role of a fixer. I've spent most of my life believing that if I didn't step in and manage the situation, things would fall apart.

I kept everything together—relationships, work, friendships, and even the emotions of the people I love. When something didn't go the way I expected, it felt like a reflection of me. When someone felt upset, when something didn't work out, or when I wasn't included, I automatically thought I had to fix it, change it, or control it.

While researching this book, I spoke with many psychologists and discovered that the urge to control things stems from a very primal place: fear. We fear exclusion, dislike, and the chaos that ensues when we don't steer the ship. It appears in various forms. We watch our kids closely, ensuring they make the "right" decisions. We influence our partner's habits, worrying that if we don't step in, they'll get it wrong. We impose our opinions on friends, convinced we know better than they do about how their lives should unfold.

I often experience that fear in my life. I feared that if I didn't make things happen, I would fade into obscurity. I feared that others wouldn't like or accept me. I worry that without my leadership, everything will fall apart. Control creates the illusion of safety. Being in control allows us to believe we can shield ourselves from pain, disappointment, and rejection.

It's merely an illusion of safety. We cannot control people or situations, no matter how hard we try. People do what they want to do. They will choose for themselves and live their own lives.

None of that "control" actually improves how you feel. It actually produces the opposite effect. Controlling people and situations won't calm your fears. It enhances them. Psychologists agree that trying to control what you can't leads to increased anxiety and stress.

I sat on that couch, stared at my phone, and realized I wasn't just trying to control what my friends thought of me—I was trying to control my own discomfort. I felt rejected, so I reacted immediately to fix the situation before I had to feel anything at all.

The Let Them Theory began to resonate with me on a much deeper level then.

Let Them: A Tool to Implement Wisdom

The Let Them Theory serves as more than a mindset hack; it draws from ancient philosophies and psychological concepts that have guided people for centuries. If you know about Stoicism, Buddhism, Detachment Theory, or Radical Acceptance, you will see that Let Them and Let Me takes these teachings and transforms them into a practical tool for enhancing your relationships and reclaiming your personal power.

Stoicism emphasizes controlling your own thoughts and actions, rather than those of others. This philosophy aligns perfectly with Let Them. It emphasizes consciously allowing others to make their own choices and live their lives without the need to manage or influence their behavior. Practicing Let Them and LetMe applies the core principle of Stoicism: Focus on yourself, because that's where your true power lies.

Buddhism and Radical Acceptance show that suffering arises from resisting reality. We often feel pain when we wish things were different than they are. The Let Them Theory empowers you to accept reality and detach from the urge to change it. You recognize that you cannot control the actions and choices of others, and by doing this, you take back your emotional freedom. This represents Radical Acceptance in its most empowering form.

Detachment Theory shows us how to create emotional distance from triggering situations. By saying Let Them, you practice emotional detachment. You establish a mental gap between your emotions and the situation at hand, enabling you to observe what's happening without being consumed by it. The outcome? You stay calm, clearheaded, and in control of your actions.

This theory differs from "letting it go." I can't let anything go—it never feels resolved. You walk away from something that bothers you, swallow your feelings, and move on. Let Them stands out. When you say Let Them, you're standing firm and choosing to engage. You are liberating yourself.

You release your grip on how things should go and allow them to unfold as they will.

Let others be who they are. Make an active, empowered choice to release control you never truly had. You free yourself from the endless cycle of stress, frustration, and emotional upheaval that comes with trying to manage everything and everyone. Let Them and Let Me empowers you to master these practices, allowing you to take control of your emotions and live a more peaceful, intentional life.

How This Works in Real Life

Consider how this impacts various aspects of your life. You sit in a meeting at work, and an exciting idea sparks in your mind. You've considered it carefully, you recognize its potential—but when you pitch it, silence fills the room. People nod politely and then move on, leaving someone else's idea to capture all the attention. You feel unseen. You begin to second-guess yourself, questioning whether you should have expressed it differently or made a greater effort to be heard.

In that moment, you can choose to let this dismissal crush you, or you can pause and say Let Them. Dismiss it. Allow them to pursue a different idea. Your idea remains valuable, regardless of their response. Your worth as a contributor remains unchanged. A different strategy may have been chosen, but that doesn't diminish the greatness of your idea. You remain the same person, equipped with the same talents and the ability to succeed. Your idea to pitch demonstrates that!

Dating works the same way. You've been texting someone, and it felt like things were heading somewhere. But then, suddenly, they disappear on you. Silence reigns, leaving questions unanswered. It really stings, right? You think about what you did wrong, replaying every conversation and trying to pinpoint where it went off the rails. I feel an overwhelming urge to text them again and seek closure. I have been there.

Here's where Let Them steps in. Allow them to reveal their true selves.

Their disrespect reflects nothing about you. Your response matters.

Quit questioning their reasons for doing this. Why do you want to be with someone who treats you this way? You do not. Stop wasting your energy on someone who has already moved on. Concentrate on what you can manage:

Process your emotions and remind yourself that you deserve someone who treats you with respect.

In both of these situations—whether it's work, dating, or anything else—when you say Let Them, you recognize what's in your control and what isn't. You choose to steady yourself and detach instead of spiraling. As I mentioned before, other people have no real power over you unless you choose to give them that power. Every time you say Let Them, you choose to take it back.

Consider me and the situation on my couch. I didn't even know my friends had gone away together. The moment I saw the photos from their trip, I reacted. I let my emotions take control. I experienced insecurity. I felt excluded. I felt inadequate. I took it a step further and told myself that I had done something wrong. That only made me feel worse.

I did this to MYSELF. My friends didn't do anything against me.

They lived their lives. They can go away. They can plan a weekend with anyone they choose. The way I reacted to their trip hurt me.

I find it crucial to understand this, and I want to dive into it with you in detail. Imagine a seesaw on a playground. It illustrates how the power dynamic between you and others shifts, rising and falling. You can apply the Let Them Theory to navigate these changes effectively.

When someone plans something without including you, you will react positively or negatively. Reacting negatively and harboring self-destructive thoughts or heavy emotions weighs you down. Your reaction tips the scales and changes the dynamic between you and someone else.

Rising above others and the situations that bother you feels empowering. People love saying Let Them because when you're up, you feel a false sense of superiority and confidence. You confront those heavy emotions and rise up. This automatically makes you feel better than someone else. You feel wiser and oddly above it all, making it easy to detach from the situation.

A touch of superiority can significantly impact your experience during an emotional spiral. That temporary feeling of power over others helps you navigate the situation, accept what's happening, and process the frustrating or painful experiences in life.

Feeling better than the friend who doesn't call you back, the lazy roommate who doesn't do their dishes, or the rude customer you deal with at work boosts your mood.

But then, that moment of Let Them is over.

Then you think... now what? You sit up there, looking down on others, and you begin to feel a bit isolated in your superiority.

After I started saying Let Them, I didn't know what to do either. Expressing it and feeling that rush of superiority felt good, and distancing from the emotion felt great. The easy part came first. I didn't know what to do next.

The danger of only saying Let Them is clear: If you keep repeating Let Them, Let Them, Let Them, you will feel more isolated. You will want to withdraw or shut down.

The old me would have handled the situation on the couch exactly like that. If I had simply stopped at the Let Them part—I can picture it now— I would have sat there in my superiority. I didn't reach out. I gossiped about them behind their backs, sought reassurance from other friends, and felt very awkward every time I saw them. I genuinely like these women and want to be friends with them!

Stop and think about a situation where you see your friends going out and doing things without you. It hurts when it happens.

Being excluded always hurts. You seek inclusion on that golf trip. You want someone to invite you over to watch the game. You plan to go away for the weekend. You love going out for drinks with your cool co-workers.

You seek to build great, fun friendships.

I want that for you as well. Let me ask you a question: How will feeling morally superior help you build those great friendships?

No, it isn't.

Letting them go eases your hurt and pain, but only for a short time. Blaming others brings a sense of satisfaction and superiority.

As your friend, I must warn you that if you only say Let Them, you will end up with few friends, limited social plans, and confusion about why the theory isn't working in your favor.

This leads me to the major discovery I made when I first started researching the theory. Let Them serves as only the first half of the equation. Don't stop there. A second, critical part of the theory is Let Me.

Your power comes from your response, not from managing others. By saying Let Me, you tap into that power and take responsibility for your next actions, thoughts, or words. Let me help you see that you control what happens next. Life becomes more fun and fulfilling when you engage with others instead of sitting alone in your superiority.

Let Me Is the Power Move

The theory works only when you state both parts. By saying Let Them, you consciously choose not to let other people's behavior affect you. When you say Let Me, you own what YOU do next.

Let Me immediately shows you what you can control, and that's what I love about it. You can control so much: your attitude, your behavior, your values, your needs, your desires, and how you choose to respond to what just happened.

It contrasts with judgment. Let Me focuses on self-awareness, compassion, empowerment, and personal responsibility.

Your friends who left are not superior to you. You are not better than them.

The Let Them Theory centers on two key ideas: Let Them and Let Me.

Allow people to live their lives, and your life will improve.

Giving up control leads to greater gains.

The Let Them Theory does not focus on superiority in any way. Balance matters. Make room for both yourself and someone else. Give others the space and grace to live their lives—and then give yourself the same.

CHAPTER 3

Shocker: Life Is Stressful

To start using the Let Them Theory quickly and effectively, rise above the countless tiny stressors you encounter daily.

Think about those never-ending notifications on your phone, the slow Internet connections, the unexpected changes in plans, the endless meetings at work, the inconsiderate behavior of others, the long lines, and the slow walkers. These small annoyances appear insignificant, but they hold more weight than you think.

I understand that people can be annoying, and you have a lot to manage.

Modern life feels like a series of relentless challenges—each one chipping away at your energy and increasing your stress. Letting it get to you is not just easy; it's foolish.

Other adults' behavior is beyond your control, and worrying about it weakens your power. Don't let stupid things or rude people drain your life force; doing so will prevent you from reaching your full potential.

Your time and energy stand as your most valuable resources. In the next few chapters, you will discover how to apply the Let Them Theory to shield yourself from the unnecessary stress that others bring into your life.

Stop and ask yourself: Why let a long line at the coffee shop ruin your day? What makes traffic put you in a bad mood? What makes you feel overwhelmed when someone interrupts you during an important task? What makes the person talking loudly on their phone in public irritate you? Why does a family member's unsolicited advice come across as a personal attack? Why does another person's slow pace in a busy walkway make you feel rushed?

I experience that as well. I visited my favorite garden center the other day to pick up some plants. The cashier moved slowly.

Only two lanes opened, and about five people waited in each.

Beep! Beep! Beep!

I started to feel agitated. I needed to get home for a meeting. I turned to the person behind me, shook my head, and said, "Can you believe this?"

I hesitated. I told myself to let them go instead. The effect occurred immediately. I became gentler. Did it make the cashier faster? No.

It achieved something better. This habit shielded me from letting little things turn into big stressors in my daily life. The 10 extra minutes this line took didn't negatively impact the rest of my day, but getting agitated and annoyed about something I couldn't control definitely would. Why stress over things you can't control or that don't truly matter? How can something so small have such a large impact on you?

Allowing the world around you to impact your emotional state and peace of mind makes you a prisoner to these external forces. You allow trivial nonsense to dictate your mood, drain your motivation, and steal your focus. Greek philosopher Epictetus famously stated, "It's not what happens to you, but how you react to it that matters." What does it mean? Your personal power lies in your reactions.

Responding differently to annoying and stressful situations every day will change your life. You give away your power when you waste your time and energy on things that don't matter or when you burn up over things beyond your control.

This problem is huge. I didn't, either.

Managing your stress is hard because you automatically react to what happens around you, causing your entire body to go on edge. You get swept up in the emotion, and before you know it, you send the text you regret. You say things in the heat of the moment that you don't really mean. You stand in a long line of people, feeling the anger and annoyance build, even though you wish they wouldn't.

Your reaction to stressful and irritating situations can create significant problems in your daily life. You cannot control what happens around you, but you can control your response to it. This is most evident at an airport. To feel stressed, just go to one.

The Airport Stress Test

The check-in process, security lines, and the chaos of weather delays can drive anyone crazy. Missing baggage, crowds at the gates before boarding, tight connections, and rerouting add to the stress. By the time you board, all the overhead space might be gone, and long lines at the rental car counter only heighten the frustration. The potential stressors are limitless.

Let's use this fact as an example to clarify what you can control and what you can't. Keep in mind the fundamental law of human nature: You cannot control what others say, think, or do.

Whenever you attempt to, you diminish your power. Focus on what you say, think, or do. You stay in control this way.

No matter what happens on the plane or at the airport, you still hold the power.

A few months ago, I sat on a plane, and the guy right behind me coughed as if it were his last day on earth. Do you recognize that deep, chest hack that will surely spread illness to everyone nearby?

I didn't think anything of it at first, but as it went on and on, and he began clearing his throat and coughing repeatedly, annoyance crept in.

I flew to an event to give a speech, and over the next couple of weeks, I spoke at several big events. I cannot afford to get sick and lose my voice.

I turned around and looked through the crack between the seats. I saw him cough openly into the air, as if no one else was on this plane. I wondered if this guy would actually make me sick. He acts so selfishly and rudely. I won't get sick. I weighed my options.

Passive-aggressive behavior won't solve anything. I huffed and puffed in my seat, glaring at him between the cracks, trying to make evil-eye contact. He either didn't pick up on my clues or simply didn't care.

I thought about flagging down the flight attendant to complain, but he sat right there, so he'd hear me, and that felt really weird. I turned around and asked him politely, "Sir, could you please cover your mouth?"

An awkward pause occurred.

He nodded and then coughed openly for the rest of the plane ride. I know this because I kept turning around and looking through the crack between the seats. You clearly feel bad for the guy. He doesn't want to be sick. Coughing is unavoidable when the urge strikes.

In the heat of the moment, my annoyance grew stronger. Stress overwhelmed me, ruining my mood and making it impossible to get any work done.

This example shows how events around you can stress you out, negatively impact your body, and hijack your brain.

Your Brain on Stress

I interviewed Dr. Aditi Neurukar, a physician at Harvard Medical School and author of The 5 Resets: Rewire Your Brain and Body for Less Stress and More Resilience, while researching this book.

Dr. Aditi served as the medical director of Harvard's Beth Israel Deaconess Hospital's integrative medicine program. She built a substantial clinical practice in stress management, employing evidence-based, integrative approaches to enhance her patients' well-being.

Dr. Aditi states, "You underestimate how much stress impacts your life."

Dr. Aditi explains that stress leads you to doubt yourself, procrastinate, burn out, doom scroll, and struggle with comparison. Stress causes trouble with focusing, feeling happy, and taking care of yourself.

If your inner critic is louder than ever, you struggle with procrastination, feel constantly tired, can't stop scrolling on your phone, or have trouble disconnecting from work, stress is the cause. Dr. Aditi explained that stress extends far beyond the tension felt in the body. Your brain experiences stress as a physiological state. Understanding this is crucial because stress hijacks the functioning of your brain. Dr. Aditi explained that your prefrontal cortex normally controls your actions.

Your brain manages your daily activities. You can plan, organize, remember things, and guide your decision-making with it. Leverage this part of your brain to become the best version of yourself.

The moment you feel stressed by the guy coughing on the plane, the long line, or the test results you're waiting for, your brain triggers a stress response. Your important prefrontal cortex loses control, and so do you.

The amygdala houses your stress response in a different part of your brain. Dr. Aditi described the amygdala as a small, almond-shaped structure deep in the brain, located between the ears. People refer to it as our 'reptilian brain,' and it stands as one of the oldest structures in the human brain. Your stress response resides there.

When someone mentions the "fight, flight, or freeze response," they refer to your "stress response." This means that during stress, your amygdala takes control. This causes rash decision-making and leads to more impulsive behaviors.

Your prefrontal cortex drives most of your actions when life is normal and you feel good. You can logically think through the pros and cons of situations and make well-thought-out decisions. You can choose how to respond.

Whenever something happens that makes you feel stressed, you and I get in trouble because our bodies and brains respond automatically. Your amygdala takes control automatically. This part of your brain has one job: it ensures your survival and self-preservation.

Your brain and body enter fight or flight mode, functioning effectively in this stressed state for only brief durations. Reset to normal functioning, where your prefrontal cortex takes control, and you feel calm and confident again. What happens when you don't reset?

The Real Reason You Are Exhausted All the Time

Dr. Aditi reports that 7 out of 10 people currently live in a chronic state of stress. I was one of them. Living in a state of chronic stress locks you in a constant fight or flight mode. Your amygdala hums in the background, always active.

Dr. Aditi explained that when you're stressed, you feel like you're in survival mode, and from a neurological standpoint, your brain actually enters survival mode. Your goals, your dreams, your best self, and your ability to be patient and nonreactive all vanish in an instant.

That's why you need to solve this problem and stop letting others create unnecessary stress in your life. Too much is at stake.

Live a good life; don't let survival mode hold you back.

Finish that project this weekend by overcoming your stress and avoiding procrastination.

Have more fun! You won't allow yourself to enjoy it if you can't disconnect from work.

Be more present and connected to your spouse. You will struggle to do this if you remain constantly stressed.

The life you've always wanted stands before you, but you will never reach for it while your inner critic keeps telling you not to. Stress poses a major problem, and now is the time to tackle it.

Hacking Your Stress Response

I asked Dr. Aditi how to reset our brain to normal functioning.

The first step is understanding what stress actually is, empowering you in these situations.

Learning that stress involves your body and brain switching between two functions was a revelation for me. I feel empowered knowing I can easily switch back to normal functioning using the Let Them Theory.

Isn't it amazing that you can live your life without letting everything around you stress you out? It's amazing that you can choose not to let other people's behavior become a huge problem in your life!

Next, use the Let Them Theory to reset your stress response. Imagine it as an on-off switch—a small lever you pull in your brain whenever stress arises.

When you say Let Them, you signal to your brain that it's okay: This isn't worth stressing about. You tell your amygdala to turn off. You reset that stress response by detaching from the negative emotion you feel.

Follow these steps: When something stresses you out, just say Let Them. Take a moment to pause. Then say Let Me and breathe deeply.

I will take another breath. Calm your stress response. Calm your body and brain. Seize control and reclaim your power.

This change may seem small, but it will transform you into a different person. Using Let Them and Let Me helps you catch your stress response and empowers you to choose your words, thoughts, and actions instead of letting your emotions take control. Stop sending rage texts, snapping at your loved ones, and wasting hours crafting emails at work.

Not every email requires a response, and not every conversation needs your input—you don't always have to have the last word.

You'll notice that many things that used to trigger you no longer deserve your time and energy. As you react less to your surroundings using Let Me, you'll feel more in control.

Dr. Aditi stated that deep breaths scientifically lower your stress response. As you breathe in fully, the air expands your belly and stimulates the vagus nerve. This nerve sends a message directly to your brain that says, "We can calm down."

Say "Let Me" and reset your stress response—you regain control and choose how to respond intentionally.

Own Your Reactions, Take Your Power Back

Let's return to my experience on the plane, where the guy behind me keeps coughing. I feel my stress levels rising, and I struggle to concentrate on my work. It's as if I'm a caged animal, trapped in my seat.

How can you apply the Let Them Theory to make someone stop coughing?

You do not. Let them cough. Allow them.

I understand. Listen to me. Yes, it stressed me out. Yes, I found him rude for not covering his mouth. I worried about getting sick.

Let's return to control: What can I control in this situation? I couldn't control another person's coughing. I could only control my response to the coughing.

When you focus on what you can't control, you create stress for yourself. When you focus on what you can control, you become powerful. This leads me to another important point: Who is responsible for my health and preventing me from getting sick?

This stranger on a plane, or me?

I. I take charge of my health. This guy doesn't have to stop coughing just because I want him to. I must respond in a way that takes care of my needs. You are thinking about something specific.

Shouldn't everyone cover their mouth? Everyone should wash their hands. Everyone should follow basic guidelines of decency. They should, but many people don't.

Trying to manage someone else or a situation beyond your control only causes more stress. I might get mad. I can keep turning around. I might yell at the flight attendant. I might feel frustrated and yell at the guy, but what would that accomplish? Isn't a more obvious and powerful solution right in front of me?

I offer you a pragmatic and strategic approach to life.

I chose not to get enraged in my seat. I let him cough, and then I focused on the simple actions I could take to protect myself.

I will cover my nose and mouth with my scarf, I thought. I will put my headphones on to drown out the coughing. I did that. I pulled my scarf over my nose and mouth and cranked up the music in my headphones.

We solved the problem.

When you say Let Them, you recognize that you lack control over this stressful situation. By saying Let Me, you follow Dr. Aditi's advice and focus on what you can control: your response to stressful situations.

Dr. Aditi confirmed, "the Let Them Theory provides a sigh of relief for your stressed brain." You reclaim control over your anxious thoughts, allowing your brain and body to escape survival mode and return to thriving.

This matters, and here's why. When you let stress take over, you hand your power to others.

This guy used to stress me out in the past. I would get zero work done, feel exhausted by the time the plane lands, and then call my husband to complain about this idiot who ruins my entire flight. I would have shared the story over dinner that night with the clients who hired me to speak at the event. I could go on and on about how "infuriating" this situation is for me. All of this left me feeling even more stressed, more worked up, and more drained.

I explain this in detail to show you what a problem this is. Letting other people stress you out surrenders your power to things that either don't matter or are beyond your control. It often spirals into other areas of your life for hours, weeks, and even years.

To achieve your goals, be more present, feel more confident, and be happier, stop letting other people stress you out. In life, you can control some things, while others remain beyond your control. Some situations will be fair, while others will not. You decide what stresses you out and how long it lasts.

Dr. Aditi's research shows that learning to protect your energy enhances your mood, mindset, health, focus, and your ability to disconnect and unplug. This is one reason many people get the words Let Them tattooed on their bodies shortly after discovering the theory.

Your peace deserves protection. A certain kind of confidence arises when you know that others can't disrupt your peace.

Let's elevate it.

A stranger coughs on a plane, creating a straightforward situation. You will get off the plane and move on with your life, making it easy to use the Let Them Theory then.

What should you do when it's unclear what the right response is? How do you apply the theory when stress arises from something larger, such as your job?

CHAPTER 4

Allow Them to Stress You Out

How can you practice Let Them and Let Me when faced with something or someone that triggers your stress response daily? Research shows that work ranks as the top cause of life stress for most people, and your manager influences your mental health just as much as your spouse does.

I know you understand that while work can be rewarding, it also comes with a lot of stress. Meetings at 4 p.m. on Fridays, rude customers, passive-aggressive emails, a micromanaging boss, work that you don't enjoy, feelings of being unappreciated, a lack of advancement opportunities, false promises, surprise layoffs, and being understaffed with extra work—it's always something.

If you're like me and have started your own business or are working to be a good manager, just double that list.

How can you apply the Let Them Theory to prevent work from stressing you out?

Imagine you've been doing a great job, hitting all your numbers, and going above and beyond, yet your boss isn't promoting you.

When you ask for an update, you receive the typical response that "the company's profits are down this year" and "my hands are tied," along with the insincere compliment that "you add so much value to this team." It's disappointing.

You experience frustration, discouragement, powerlessness, hostility, or demoralization. Dr. Aditi explains why she is witnessing record numbers of burnout at this moment:

Workers experience a state of chronic stress at work. She added that your stress at work isn't changing, so you need to change your approach to dealing with it.

I remember feeling exactly that way when I found myself in that situation. Your need for a paycheck to cover your bills adds to your stress and sense of powerlessness.

Even though work feels overwhelming right now, you hold power.

How can you apply the Let Them Theory to persuade your boss to grant you the promotion you deserve?

You do not. Allow them to lead you on.

It's tough to hear, but it's true. Indeed, it's unfair. Absolutely, you earned that promotion. You absolutely have every right to feel angry about it.

Let me ask you this: Who takes charge of YOUR career?

You are right.

You can't control whether your boss promotes you, gives you a raise, or moves you to the cubicle closer to the window. Your hard work and the compliments you've received don't change the fact that the decision rests with them.

If you find yourself in a situation where you've put in the effort, had the conversation, asked for the salary increase, and hit your numbers, yet you're still waiting for that promotion, title change, or new desk, it's time to stop being mad and decide what action to take next.

Guess what? Letting your emotions take control will drive you crazy. Letting the stress of this situation take over prevents you from thinking strategically about your next move.

Don't allow the stress of this to cloud your judgment. Be smart about how you respond. Allow me. Your power lies there.

If something at work is beyond your control and you've done everything possible to influence it, stop wasting time trying to change the situation. It's even dumber to let it constantly stress you out. You know better than that. Your life and the possibilities within it always exceed your current job.

You are always moving forward. You're lying to yourself. Leave a job, a relationship, a living situation, a date, an interview, or a conversation whenever you want.

Instead, you sit there with your boss Steve, flipping him off every time the Zoom meeting ends.

Leave any job that frustrates, demoralizes, or stresses you. You should not. Allow them to lead you on.

Now, we move on to the Let Me part. Quit dwelling on your current situation and begin seeking a better opportunity. An amazing job with a kickass boss, a better salary, and a desk next to a window awaits your discovery. Many companies exist on this planet, and countless bosses would be thrilled to help you advance your career.

I will go get it.

Finding a job can be challenging. Absolutely. Will it take forever? Absolutely. Do you feel anxious about updating your resume? Absolutely. Does networking and getting out there feel intimidating? Absolutely. You own your career, and you wield more power here than you realize. Now is the moment to take action.

I will choose to spend my weekends differently. Rather than venting at the bars with friends and grumbling about work, focus your time and energy on finding the job you deserve. Yes, you might spend six months pursuing something amazing, but those six months will pass regardless of whether you take action or chase your goals.

Consider this: If you remain in that job, who shapes your future?

Exactly. Steve, your boss. Update your resume, start networking, and go on some interviews. Now, you're in control! That's correct.

YOU.

Act like a toddler and call your boss every name in the book, but the harsh truth is that you're to blame—you choose to stay in a job that makes you miserable.

That's your responsibility. Do you want to know what else is on you? Your excuses for not searching for another job are unconvincing. You possess far more power than you realize. Now is the moment to begin taking action.

You Control Your Next Move

I want to address in greater detail how you can determine the right response for yourself when you say Let Me. The Let Them part stands out clearly.

When you say Let Them, you stop controlling what someone else does. When you say Let Me, you take charge of how you respond to it, which isn't always clear.

Each situation differs, and learning to choose which responses deserve your time and energy will transform your life. This story will help you understand how to choose the right response for you.

Recently, I took our dogs for a walk at a popular spot in a local state park. A local park ranger stopped to pet my two dogs and say hello as I pulled into the parking lot. While we chatted, he reminded me to keep the dogs on a leash and pick up their poop. He noted that many complaints arose about dogs running free and owners not cleaning up after them. They were reaching a point where they might close the trails to dogs.

I thanked him for sharing that information and assured him that I am not "one of those people" and will follow the rules. I walked down the trail and saw a person 100 feet ahead of me. Their dog ran off the leash, darting around and jumping on people.

I began to feel annoyed. The stress response surged, and my amygdala activated. I no longer enjoyed my walk in the woods. I focused like a laser on this dog and its owner, growing more and more annoyed that this was exactly what the park ranger had warned about. This one idiot threatened to get us all banned from being here.

I said Let Them, and it worked for the first five times. Her dog crouched in the middle of the trail and went number two. I watched in horror as the owner kicked some leaves over it instead of picking it up in a doggy bag and removing it.

That was the moment. I shifted from feeling stressed to declaring myself the dog police in just five seconds. This highlights an important aspect of using the theory. You will respond to every situation in a unique and different way each time.

Some days, I simply lack the energy to chase this woman down, hand her a doggie bag, ask her to pick it up, explain the implications of what's going on, and request that she do her part.

Some days, I will run like an Olympic sprinter, chase her down, and achieve that goal.

I will have moments when I shrug my shoulders, say Let Them, and recognize it's not worth my time and energy. When I reach the point where the dog has made its mess, I will be the bigger person and pick it up with a baggie. I'll smear it all over her car in the parking lot (that last part is a joke).

I prefer not to pick up after others, yet I take pride in being someone who cares about keeping public spaces tidy for everyone's enjoyment. I enjoy making sure I improve places I visit. I love taking charge and acting like a leader, even when it's not my responsibility.

Some days, I will decide that the best course of action is to turn around, walk back to the parking lot, find that park officer, wait with them until the woman returns, and report her to the ranger so he can handle the situation.

All of these Let Me options are available to you and me.

While you read, you might have considered other options. Every situation is different, but one thing stays constant: You always choose how to respond.

I can't stop that lady from letting her dog poop in the middle of the trail, but I can decide how to respond to it. I choose who I am and how I show up, and that feels incredibly powerful.

Your feelings, current life circumstances, available time, the importance of the issue, your values, and the most effective approach will shape each situation differently.

Let Me offers you the chance to place your time, energy, and values at the core of your life. You choose what deserves your attention and what doesn't. How do you determine what's best for you?

Especially in a highly stressful situation? That's a great question.

In these stressful moments, I find it helpful to say Let Them, pause, and consider: Will this bother me in an hour? Will this bother me in a week? Does this only bother me right now?

If I still think about it an hour from now, I will take action. If it will matter in a week or a year, then I must take action. This lady and her dog would bother me every single time I walked my dog at that state park.

You often know what is right for you. This brings me to the next example, which perfectly follows poop: politics.

Recent research shows that most people feel very stressed about the current state of world politics. I sense it as well. How can you not?

We live in a moment of intense polarization, where the stakes feel high, and people appear distant, often angry or scared about the current situation (or both).

Many people struggle to engage in civil conversations with those who hold different viewpoints, as few of us genuinely invest the time to understand the other person's perspective.

Given how stressful politics can be at the local, state, national, and global level, many people throw their hands up in the air, disengage, and feel powerless to change the state of things.

How can you apply the Let Them Theory to transform politics at local, national, or global levels?

You do not. The school board decided already. The Senate voted.

The two candidates are running. The voters have made their choice. The courts have it tied up. Allow them. What just happened is unchangeable.

I never said you couldn't change the future. Does it feel overwhelming? Absolutely. Does it seem like it won't matter? Absolutely.

Just do it. I will stay engaged and vocal on the issues I care about and take action to change the future of my local, national, and global politics. Take action and clean up the mess that you see instead of waiting for someone else to do it.

Be the one everyone else is waiting for if it matters. Make the change you want to see. Let Me holds the power.

I remind myself of what Professor Margaret Mead said: "Never doubt that a small group of thoughtful, committed citizens can change the world; indeed, it's the only thing that ever has."

One person can make the right choice. If it bothers you enough, you are that person. We can always do something. Make a difference. If it doesn't matter enough for you to get involved, then stop complaining about it. It stresses you out. While you learn, that seems unwise. Words hold little value. If it truly bothers you, invest your time and energy in changing it.

Time and time again, no matter the situations and circumstances in which you apply the Let Them Theory, you discover that regardless of the size of the problem or the level of stress, you can always take action and adjust your attitude to improve the situation.

Let Me holds great power. You cannot control everyone around you, the world at large, or what people do at the park, but you can always control your responses—what you say, think, or do—and that's where true power lies.

The more you tap into that power, the more you see how you've sabotaged your own happiness and given away your power. You didn't even know it, just like I didn't. Your time and energy matter greatly. The Let Them Theory emphasizes this and empowers you to choose wisely about where to invest your time and energy. This means engaging in difficult conversations instead of remaining silent.

Being assertive doesn't mean being a doormat and allowing others to walk all over you; it also doesn't require you to pick up everyone's dog poop or run for political office.

You choose what impacts you and to what extent. You choose what you participate in and what you don't.

You decide when a job, relationship, or issue is worth fighting for and when it's time to walk away. You choose, and that is why you control what happens next.

Let's summarize what you learned about managing stress. You let other people create unnecessary stress in your life. The Let Them Theory empowers you to protect your energy by refusing to let minor irritations dictate your life, enabling you to concentrate on what truly matters.

1. **Problem**: Other people will engage in activities throughout the day that bother you, annoy you, or stress you out. It happens. It's beyond your control. Allowing someone else's behavior to stress you out gives them power over you. You feel drained, lacking time and energy for yourself.

2. **Truth**: Your body automatically responds to stress. You feel yourself getting annoyed. Frustration will arise. The anger and agitation will hit you. Emotions rise up inside of you, and you can't control them.

Learn how to reset your stress response so your emotions don't hijack you.

3. **Solution**: Apply the Let Them Theory to shield yourself from the stress others have caused you. You control your response to another person's behavior, to the annoying situation, and to the emotions you feel.

When you say Let Them, you decide not to let other people's behavior stress you out or bother you. By saying Let Me, you reset your stress response and take charge of how you respond.

CHAPTER 5

Allow Others to Form Negative Opinions About You

In her poem "The Summer Day," poet Mary Oliver poses this question: "Tell me, what is it you plan to do with your one wild and precious life?"

I'm not sure how you would respond to Mary Oliver's question, but I can tell you this: Whatever you decide to do, others will definitely have their opinions on it.

In the next few chapters, you will discover how to apply the Let Them Theory to prevent others' opinions from hindering your pursuit of what you desire and to unlock the full potential of your one wild and precious life.

This problem is huge. I didn't either. People often put on a facade that they don't care what others think, but the reality is that everyone does.

People will form negative opinions about you, and you cannot change this fact. Allowing your fear of what others think to stop you from pursuing your desires makes you a prisoner to their opinions.

This fear influences every part of your life. You procrastinate. You start to doubt yourself. Perfectionism paralyzes you. You overthink because of it.

This is where it ends. Now is the moment to empower people to think freely. Allow them. Set yourself free and let me help you make small moves boldly and unapologetically that will transform your entire life over time.

The Let Them Theory served as a huge wake-up call for me. I realized I was worried about other people's opinions, but I didn't understand the extent of the problem until I began saying Let Them. Let them judge. Let them disapprove. Allow them to express their opinions. Allow them to entertain negative thoughts. Let them discuss me when I'm not around.

You navigate life using other people's opinions as your guide. You choose the left or right turn based on your anticipation of others' thoughts or comments, instead of making the turn you truly desire.

Navigating your life while trying to predict what others think and say about you leads you to give away your power.

Stop overthinking every move you make. Just let them think whatever they want. Freeing yourself of this burden changes your life. Keep in mind the fundamental law of human nature: You cannot control what another adult says, does, or thinks. Attempt it, and you'll regret it. Letting them think what they want improves your life.

Imagine giving yourself permission to live your life fully, while allowing others to think whatever they choose about it. Imagine pouring your time and energy into your hobbies, your habits, your happiness.

What change would you make without worrying about judgment? What do you secretly desire but hesitate to acknowledge?

Which belief makes you feel hesitant to express yourself more openly? What have you held back from trying because you haven't done it before? What challenge, race, or adventure have you secretly longed to pursue? What do you want to happen at work that you hesitate to ask for? Which conversation are you avoiding? Which picture are you eager to post?

The last one really resonates with me.

Welcome to the Greatest Challenge You Face in Life

Ten years ago, I started my journey as a motivational speaker. I entered the speaking industry as a newcomer. Like many new businesses, there was no money in the beginning. I will reach out to small women's conferences and pitch myself to speak for free to get started and get my foot in the door.

When you start a business, manage a side hustle, or try to make money online through social media, you likely find yourself putting in a lot of work with no return in the beginning.

I felt frustrated as a year passed. I improved onstage, and audiences grew larger, yet my bank account shrank. What's the reason? I worked a full-time job during the week and took on these speaking gigs for free on the weekends.

I wrote in the Introduction of this book about the time when my husband and I struggled with massive financial debt. This situation motivated me to find ways to make money doing this.

I sought advice from experienced speakers on how to start getting paid, and I recommend you do the same in any business, venture, or side hustle you dream of launching.

Each business possesses a formula. Take action on it. People often get hung up on the belief that they need to be different. You're afraid others will think you copied them. Your fear of what others think holds you back from following the most obvious, easiest, and most proven path to success.

Let them believe you copied them. You did. They copied the formula from someone else. They did. Formulas exist because they deliver results consistently. You make it unique by putting yourself into the formula. Don't create something from scratch. Utilize the formula and make it work for you.

The experienced speakers advised me to do exactly that. Successful speakers consistently do three things. Until you do these things, you aren't truly in the speaking game.

They instructed me to do the following:

1. Create a straightforward website featuring photos of you on stage, along with a description of your keynote and the key takeaways.

2. Collect testimonials from several event planners at past events where you spoke and display them on the website.

Next, the most important point:

3. Begin sharing your thoughts on speaking online. Transform your social media into a powerful marketing tool. Share photos from events. Share content that connects to your speech. Share photos featuring the event planners who hire you. People find you through social media. Social media shows that you actively participate in this industry. Social media drives people to that one-page website where they can book you.

This is the formula. Follow it, and you will begin to receive payment. With that advice in hand, I knew exactly what to do. The stakes were really high. I needed the money to free my family from debt. I clearly understood what I needed to do.

Did I follow the formula? Nope. I created a website. I requested testimonials and added them to the website. Did I post on social media? No.

My social media served a personal purpose back then. Photos of my kids, pictures from family trips, and selfies with friends filled it. My followers included friends, former classmates, and family members. I never posted anything about my desire to become a motivational speaker or the fact that I had been doing it for free for over a year.

If you've ever wanted to use social media to launch a business, promote a new aspect of your life, or share your art, you know how challenging it is to look at your account filled with personal photos and decide to transform it into a marketing channel.

I spent TWO YEARS before I began posting about my business on social media. What's the reason?

Because I Was Afraid of What People Would Think

Who did you fear, Mel? My friends are here.

I feared that if I shifted from posting photos of my kids and family gatherings to sharing images of me speaking at conferences, people would judge me.

Who does she believe she is? Who is hiring her to speak? What could she possibly say? That's a fake.

I posted. I would thumb through my photos from the event and select one or two. Then fear would kick in. I drafted a caption and felt worried about others' negative opinions: Does this sound too arrogant? Does this caption convey professionalism? Will people unfollow me if I post this? Do my friends think I'm full of myself? Should I start a new account from the beginning?

I convinced myself that it wasn't worth it to post. Do you want to know why? I burned through so much energy crafting the perfect, most compelling, and marketable image and caption—something that promoted me and ensured no one thought a negative thought—that I exhausted myself.

I crafted hundreds of draft posts. They sat there in my drafts for years. When I finally felt the jolt of confidence to post, I left it up for five minutes and checked it obsessively. If the likes didn't meet my expectations or the comments fell short of my hopes, I deleted it.

This fear held me back from marketing my business, which I wanted to turn into my full-time career, for years. I prioritized other people's opinions over my own ability to succeed in life. Discuss how you relinquish your power.

Looking back at it now makes me sad.

I held myself back from taking the actions that could have helped me achieve my goals, make more money, get out of debt, buy nice things for my kids, and attract many more clients quickly. That's stupid.

It's clearly foolish. You likely face the same fear when it comes to "putting yourself out there."

If you're censoring yourself, it's because you fear people's opinions about your business, your art, your music, your videos, or even a photo of you in a bathing suit. You cover up your acne and insist on standing "on your good side" in every photo. This is the same reason you avoid speaking up at meetings. You fear looking bad online and sounding bad at work. You fear what others will think if they see the real you.

When you edit what you post, stay silent in class or at work, or hide in the back of the group photo, you engage in self-rejection.

You tell yourself that you're not good enough. Constantly questioning, editing, deleting, overthinking, and asking others, "Does this look good?" magnifies your self-doubt. You want to know the crazy part? You are causing this for yourself. I also did.

Much of the advice on this topic falls short. Many people advise you to simply "stop caring" about others' opinions. No one shows you how to do it. Now is the moment for a new approach. With the Let Them Theory, you adopt a revolutionary approach to squashing this fear once and for all: You give people the freedom to think negative thoughts about you.

This idea radically enhances your confidence, liberates your self-expression, and propels you into a whole new chapter of your life.

Allow people to form their own negative opinions about you.

Allow them. It works effectively. Science drives it.

You Have Zero Control over Someone Else's Opinion of You

You cannot control someone else's thoughts. Therefore, fearing what others think or trying to control their thoughts wastes your time.

Stop being consumed by or trying to control what other people think about you. Only then will you feel in control of your life, your feelings, your thoughts, and your actions.

Let me repeat: Adults will form negative opinions about you—regardless of your actions. What's the reason? Adults can think whatever they want.

You cannot control what someone else thinks, either physically or neurologically. On average, a human being generates around 70,000 thoughts each day. Many of these are random and remain beyond our control. It's ludicrous to waste your energy worrying about what others think or trying to change their opinions.

Half the thoughts that pop into your own mind remain beyond your control.

Why do you believe you can control what appears in someone else's? You cannot. Scientists find it impossible. The Let Them Theory revolutionizes the way we think.

Stop fearing other people's opinions; let them think what they want. Assume people will think negative thoughts about you. People have negative thoughts about you.

This is typical.

People who love you think bad thoughts about you every day! Every day, I struggle with negative thoughts about the people I love! This is typical. I'll go first to prove it.

My husband usually wakes up and lets out a huge fart. You disgust me. I love Chris more than anyone else on the planet. I constantly think negatively about him and hold bad opinions.

My dog does the same thing. At 5 p.m., my dog, Homie, becomes incredibly annoying because he knows it's dinnertime. He follows me around, pants like crazy, and jumps up on me. I think he is a giant pain in the rear end and needs to chill. I still love him.

My oldest daughter, Sawyer, co-authored this book with me. She has a strong need for control, and when things aren't perfect, she becomes overbearing and intense. She dives into an OCD cleaning spiral that stresses everyone else out. I still love her.

Whenever our middle daughter, Kendall, FaceTimes me from Los Angeles, she always seems to be wearing a new outfit. She handles her money irresponsibly, and she definitely doesn't need more clothes. I still love her.

Our son, Oakley, is truly perfect. I'm just joking. During the first hour he is awake, he avoids making eye contact and speaking to others. He is rude. I still love him.

I asked my children to describe some adjectives they think about me. People describe me as messy, disorganized, loud, overfriendly, all-over-the-place, controlling, always late, and a know-it-all. They also have many opinions about how much I share online about our life. They still love me.

Sawyer wanted you to know that writing this book with me nearly drove her to sever parental rights due to the number of times I completely blew up the manuscript—for context, this is version 11.0.

Here's why I'm sharing this with you. Everyone holds critical opinions about both the people they love and complete strangers. Life presents facts.

Embrace it and accept it. Use reality to your advantage instead of trying to change it. Allow them.

Here's another truth: A negative opinion from someone doesn't mean they view you negatively overall.

I can have a negative thought about my husband while still loving him and treating him with respect and kindness, because both can coexist. You might feel annoyed by someone's behavior, yet you still love them deeply.

You feel this way about the people you love! You believe their friends influence them negatively. You believe they are overreacting. You believe their boyfriend treats them poorly. You believe their business idea will fail.

You believe they focus only on themselves. You still love them.

My point is clear: Adults will form negative opinions about you and your actions. Let them judge. Allow them to react. Let them question you.

Allow them to question the decisions you make. Allow them to be mistaken about you. Let them roll their eyes when you post videos online or when you rewrite the manuscript for the 12th time.

Stop wasting your time worrying about them. Live your life in a way that makes you proud of yourself. I will pursue what I want to do with my one wild and precious life.

This approach liberates you because you live your life and make decisions without worrying about what everyone else thinks. Letting the fear of others' opinions dictate your choices limits your potential and holds you back from pursuing what you truly want.

You procrastinate, doubt yourself, get paralyzed by perfectionism, and, most importantly, you wake up every day and avoid the work that would actually help you get ahead.

Your fear of judgment holds you back from taking any risks. Are you afraid of that? Are you worried about being judged?

If you get divorced, quit the real estate business, go back to school, cut your hair, or try out for the soccer team and get cut, everyone will have an opinion about it. They will definitely have an opinion about it. What does that mean?

This fear holds you back from trying new things, taking risks, being yourself, and making the small moves that will change your life over time. That's unfortunate.

The Let Them Theory empowers you to embrace courage. Isn't it smarter to accept reality and allow people the freedom to judge?

Don't let someone else's thoughts hold you back. You have no control over what they think, so there's no reason to fear it or let it stop you any longer. Your time holds immense value, as you have significant things to accomplish in this one wild and precious life.

Today, you will grant people the freedom to think negative thoughts about you. Allow them.

Make Decisions That Make YOU Proud

This highlights a crucial aspect of prioritizing your needs while nurturing supportive and loving relationships. It's essential to navigate life with consideration for others, avoiding a selfish or narcissistic mindset.

Focus on learning to prioritize your needs while balancing what works for you alongside the expectations and feelings of others. In life, you should stand your ground, but you also need to be mindful of others. Finding balance is essential.

You have a crazy-busy weekend ahead. Your close friend celebrates a big milestone birthday, and friends gather for a truly fun weekend of celebration.

You need to make a four-hour drive to reach the party location. You know that being there is the right decision for you. You promised your parents months ago that you would come home this weekend because your grandparents are visiting.

You want to achieve both.

You strive to be a good friend, a good child, and a good grandkid, so you drive four hours north of the city to join the Friday night festivities for your friend.

You feel glad you did.

You laugh with friends late into the night and finish a bottle of wine. You enjoy yourself immensely. You wake up at 7 a.m. the next morning. You roll out of bed, pull on your sweats, leave a note apologizing for missing the rest of the weekend, and get back in the car to drive another four hours to your parents' house to spend the weekend with your grandparents.

While you drive on the road, you feel proud of yourself for making the effort.

The birthday girl felt upset that you left. She said, "I don't know why she even bothered coming if she could only stay one night."

Allow her.

Four hours later, you arrive at your parents'—feeling a bit hungover and quite tired. You exit the car in your sweats and embrace your grandma, who beams with excitement and tears of joy fill her eyes.

You hug your mom, and she whispers in your ear, "Your grandmother was so disappointed you weren't here when she arrived last night." She adds, "We need to leave for lunch in ten minutes." Change is necessary.

Allow her.

This story demonstrates two key points: Even when you bend over backward to please everyone and make it work, that won't guarantee others will think positively. Allow them.

Second—and this is the most important point—don't become the person who bends over backward to please everyone. I am that person now. I felt depleted and believed nothing I did was ever good enough.

Now that I understand the Let Them Theory, I actively strive to create my own happiness. I will explain.

Making a herculean effort to attend your friend's birthday party and visit your grandparents brings a sense of pride in yourself. Skip your friend's birthday to make them believe you are a good friend. Attend your friend's birthday to show that you care.

Stay away from home to avoid making your mother happy by visiting your grandparents. Visit your grandparents at home; it brings YOU joy to prioritize your family.

When you act in a way that fills you with pride, the opinions of others hold no weight. You will make them mad by leaving early.

You will make them mad by arriving late. Someone will always feel disappointed by your decisions. Always ensure you are not the one who feels disappointed. Don't allow guilt to dictate your choices.

Going to your parents because you feel "guilty" turns them into the villain. Choosing to go because you'd be mad at yourself if you didn't puts you in control of your decisions.

This example clearly shows how to stop worrying about what others think and let your values guide your decisions.

What happens when your opinion clashes with someone else's? What if your mom dislikes the person you plan to marry? What do you do next?

I have been there.

CHAPTER 6

How to Love Difficult People

I find it easier to apply the Let Them Theory with strangers, coworkers, and even friends, as the distance allows for some recharging after using it. Walk into your bedroom and shut the door. Go home after work. Walk off the plane.

Most of the time, you won't even realize when someone thinks negatively about you. What about family? Family impacts in unique ways. Your family stands by you for life.

Your family expresses their opinions directly and openly. They feel angry that you aren't coming home for the holidays. People constantly question why you remain single. You've ruined your life by dropping out of school, according to them. Your friend group faces their hatred. They oppose your way of living. They express their dislike for your choice of partner. Don't quit your job to start that business.

They want you to take better care of yourself, and they express this clearly.

Family often speaks more bluntly to you because they care deeply about your happiness and success. Often, when your family cares, they express it by pushing you. They express their disapproval when they don't like your friends, when they think you're headed down the wrong path, or when they wish you would take better care of yourself.

Your family often demonstrates their care for you. They desire more for you, they want you to find happiness, and they recognize all your potential as it goes to waste. However, it can easily shift from caring to controlling.

Your family has formed opinions about you since the day you were born. You have been known by them the longest. They believe they have the right to their opinions because they think they know what's best for you. This typically feels best for them.

Additionally, each family member holds expectations about one another and how the family should function. Familial relationships cut deeper than others because you have known them for a long time, and they form an interconnected system. Your family reacts more dramatically to any change you make because you are part of that family system. Your changes will create either positive or negative waves throughout the entire system.

Understanding that people will react because you belong to a long-standing network of relationships can help you navigate this situation more effectively.

I don't claim that those expectations or that system is correct. I'm stating that this is the reality. Understanding the larger context of any situation helps me stay in control of how I show up in my family.

Deciding to get a divorce from your spouse, rejecting old traditions, marrying someone outside your religion, pursuing a unique career path, or holding different political beliefs sends shock waves through the entire family system. These choices disrupt everyone's expectations and beliefs about who you are and how you should live your life.

The dynamics of stepchildren and stepparents clearly illustrate this interlocked web. This major shock hits the family system and can either strengthen or weaken it, for better or for worse.

New individuals completely disrupt all expectations for how the household runs. People often find it challenging to accept change.

Especially for the kids who must accept this change and operate as one big happy blended family.

The Let Them Theory changes the game for navigating your role as a stepparent. As the adult, you must allow them to grieve. Show them you (and your kids) pose a threat, because regardless of your good intentions, you are a threat. You compete with them for time with the parent. It is true. You seek control, just like they do. Allow them to experience their emotions. Allow them to spend time alone with their parent. They don't have to like you. Allow them.

Always remember that stepchildren need your understanding, grace, and compassion. They learn to accept a new adult in their life while grieving the loss of the family they wanted.

This is typical.

Understanding the larger context helps you focus on the Let Me part and operate with more grace, becoming the wise and compassionate adult. Displaying more grace and kindness creates more space for a change in the dynamic to happen.

Stepchildren and stepparents face challenging dynamics. They are not seamless at all. They also hold the potential to become much more beautiful with the Let Them Theory and a specific tool you will learn about in this chapter.

A therapist once stated at a conference, "If it weren't for families, I wouldn't have a business." Your relatives can have their opinions about family, but that doesn't give them the right to reject your choices, your individuality, or your right to love whomever you choose.

The point is not whether their opinions are right or wrong. Your relationship with their opinions matters.

What do you do when your loved ones disagree with how you live your life or who you are? I relate. Here's what you will do about it. Allow them.

Avoid attempting to change their opinion. Allow them to have it freely.

Your stepkids, sister-in-law, grandmother, and brother can think whatever they want. They can choose not to like you or the person you love. Allow them to proceed. Then, allow me to choose how to respond.

Frame of Reference

My friend Lisa Bilyeu, a bestselling author, host of the Women of Impact podcast, and co-founder of the billion-dollar nutrition company Quest Nutrition, shared the concept of Frame of Reference.

This tool helps you handle situations where someone disapproves of who you are, who you love, what you believe, or how you live your life, allowing you to navigate these challenges at a deeper level.

I've been there, and perhaps you have as well.

Our global podcast audience went wild for Frame of Reference when Lisa shared how it serves as a mindset tool that has improved her relationships. Frame of Reference means understanding the lens through which someone sees something, and it aligns perfectly with the Let Them Theory.

Here's an example from my life. I felt ecstatic and madly in love when I met my husband, Chris. When he proposed, I felt absolutely over the moon. I remember my mom not seeming as excited as I expected.

I had a conversation with her where I expressed my desire for her to feel excited for me, and I asked her to behave as if she had chosen him for me.

She said, "I didn't choose him for you, and if it were up to me, I wouldn't have, so I won't act like I did."

I felt so angry that I didn't know what to do. I wanted to keep her in my life, but I struggled to find a way to handle the situation. I am madly in love with someone I know is my soulmate, yet my mom tells me, "I would never have picked him for you," and then refuses to act excited for me.

I married Chris, but I felt the tension of disapproval beneath the dynamic between my mom and me for years. I found it hard to forget what she said. I didn't know how to release it.

Over time, the tension faded, and 30 years later, my mother loves Chris. She often jokes, "Chris, you're my favorite son-in-law" (he's also her only son-in-law).

How did I navigate this? Recently, I have used the Let Them Theory and the Frame of Reference tool to understand why she felt the way she did. This has truly transformed my relationship with my mom and enhanced my ability to support her even when I disagree with her opinion.

If I were in my mother's position, understanding her life experiences, I wouldn't want me to marry Chris either. What's the reason? Chris hails from the East Coast, and marrying him likely means I will settle there, leaving behind the Midwest and my mom and dad for good.

My mother's perspective is clear: after she left home and met my father, she never returned home again. At 17, my mom left the family farm in upstate New York to attend college in Kansas. She met my dad there, and they fell in love. At 19, she married and had me.

She and my dad didn't plan this, but it's what happened. When my dad's parents learned that my mom was pregnant with me, my grandmother told my 19-year-old mother, "I hope you didn't just ruin our son's life."

Can you picture it? Thinking about how young my parents were, living in Kansas without any family nearby, fills me with sadness.

My mom lived this experience, shaping her perspective on raising a family far from her parents and highlighting the challenges of lacking family support.

My mom and dad settled in Michigan after my dad completed his residency and medical school. Growing up, I rarely saw my grandparents or extended family because they lived so far away. Just my mom, my dad, my brother, and I were there. We stand as our own little family of four, facing the world together.

When I left home for college on the East Coast, I felt a surge of fear that I might never return home. When I met Chris in New York, who also hailed from the East Coast, my mom's biggest fear became real: I would start my life far away and never return to my small Midwestern town.

That's exactly what happened. My mom faced her biggest fear.

From my mother's perspective, she witnessed her story unfolding before her once more. I planned to move away, meet someone, and never return home.

She was right. She wanted me to marry someone from Michigan so I would settle down close to them. Thirty years ago when I met Chris, I didn't consider my mom's perspective. I felt offended and angry, concluding that she "didn't support me."

Now, I see that she supported me; she just feared losing her daughter. She loves me and wants me close by. I can give her the freedom to wish my life took a different path through the Let Them Theory, and I can also deeply understand where she is coming from.

I understand how difficult it is to watch your daughter marry someone who will take her away from you. I wouldn't select someone like that for my daughters and son either.

I don't want my daughter Sawyer to marry someone from Europe and move to Paris. If it makes her happy, she should do it. But would that be my decision? Absolutely not. This might come off as unsupportive or controlling, yet every parent can relate. I'm not saying that to control. I say that because that's how I feel. I may have a negative opinion, but I have the right to hold it. I'm sure my daughter would feel very unsupportive.

Kendall experiences the same thing. She lives in LA and might meet someone from California, leading her to settle down and raise her family there. I would see her and her kids less often than if they lived here on the East Coast.

I have that opinion, just as Sawyer can move to Paris and Kendall can choose to raise a family in LA.

My mom can have the opinion that she wouldn't choose someone from the East Coast for me. I'm glad it didn't prevent me from marrying Chris and living where we wanted to raise our family.

I feel grateful for the Let Them Theory because I understand my mom and her reluctance from 30 years ago. Grief, not judgment, filled the air. She was right. She is right. I wasn't wrong either.

We were both right. We have different frames of reference.

Her perspective helps me restore balance in our relationship.

The power struggle ended; understanding emerged.

Navigating these types of situations proves challenging because both of you believe you are right. Their lived experience shapes their belief that their opinion is correct. Your lived experience shapes your perspective, and you believe your opinion is correct.

The Let Them Theory creates space for acceptance and understanding, allowing both of our opinions to coexist as true. A deeper connection, honesty, and love exist in this space.

A remarkably mature person can detach from their emotions and step into someone else's shoes. Understanding that someone can love you while holding deeply hurtful and sometimes bigoted opinions is challenging.

When this happens in life, your response becomes a deeply personal choice. I can't advise you on how to handle judgment from a family member. I can provide you with the tools to decide how to respond to the situation.

Do you want this person in your life? The Let Them Theory creates the space for it. In my experience and through researching this book while listening to the stories of many others, I see that when you provide people the space to reach their own conclusions and focus on being your full self with love and compassion, people often change their opinions over time.

As challenging as it may seem, allow them to have their opinions and concentrate on how you will respond. This idea of stepping into someone else's Frame of Reference fascinates me. Understanding where someone comes from might not change opinions, but it deepens the connection as you navigate your relationship.

You create space for two things to be true at once, and that space allows love to exist. I understand—it's easy to feel irritated or offended by your parents. Blaming them is simple.

Feeling frustrated and annoyed with the dynamics of your siblings, divorced parents, in-laws, stepparents, or adult children is common. Choosing not to understand their perspectives is easy.

Decide whether you will accept people as they are, especially your family or stepfamily, or create the distance you need. One person can change how they show up in a family, and the entire system can improve. You are that person.

I love the Let Them Theory because whenever you improve yourself, you enhance all your relationships, especially with family. The impact has affected my own family.

The things that used to bother me no longer stress me out. I refuse to get sucked into the drama. I maintain laser focus on how I show up and live my life to make myself proud.

I have determined that having a close relationship with my family is important to me. Wasting my time and energy on their stress or attempting to control situations beyond my reach is pointless.

You have limited time with your loved ones. Eventually, you will understand that your parents won't always be around, and that they are experiencing life as humans for the first time as well.

Individuals can connect with you only to the extent that they understand themselves. Many people avoid therapy, ignore their issues, and choose not to confront them.

Allow them. Don't settle for less than what you deserve from your parents. Make your family life real and authentic, not a fairy tale. They make the most of the resources and life experiences available to them. You choose what happens next.

I don't intend to justify any bad actions that occur. You deserve better, and I'm not denying that. Everyone deserves to feel seen, supported, and loved, especially by their family.

Most human beings have not taken the time to understand themselves, heal their past, or manage their emotions. If they haven't taken care of themselves, they can't take care of you and show up the way you deserve.

Allow them. Recognizing that gives you a choice in your life. Allow your family to be themselves. Your dad isn't changing. Your mom remains the same. Your siblings remain the same. Your in-laws remain the same. You can only change yourself.

When you say Let Them, you see your family exactly as they are for the first time in your life, perhaps. Humans exist. You cannot control what happened. You cannot control who they are. From this point forward, you control what you do.

Accept the reality of your situation; it doesn't mean you surrender to it. Reclaim your power and shape your future. Discover how to allow adults to be themselves and embrace people for who they are. Decide how to make the best of it, and your family dynamics will improve.

This acceptance enables you to view your family with compassion, and more importantly, it empowers you to recognize yourself as an individual with your own unique Frame of Reference and path in life.

Next, you move to the second part: Let Me. I will determine what kind of relationship I want to create, based on the person I aim to be and the values I hold.

Spend time with your family because it matters to you, not out of guilt. Defining your own traditions may upset your family. That means being someone who always makes the effort, even when others do not return it.

It means saying "I love you," "I understand," or "I forgive you" for the first time.

That means having the hard conversations you have avoided due to fear of their opinions or judgment. Free yourself from guilt and make some changes. It may mean separating yourself because you no longer accept less than you deserve. It may require you to go all in while you still have time.

Let's summarize what you learned about fearing other people's opinions. Your fear of other people's opinions controls you right now. The Let Them Theory shows you how to reclaim your life from the influence of others' opinions, empowering you to live in a way that fills you with pride.

1. Problem: You give other people's opinions too much power.

Letting the fear of others' opinions dictate your choices limits your potential and holds you back from pursuing what you truly want. This fear leads you to procrastinate, doubt yourself, become paralyzed by perfectionism, and, most importantly, abandon your dreams.

2. Truth: No matter what you do, people will form negative opinions about you. It happens. Allow them. It's beyond your control. Letting someone else's opinion distract or consume you wastes your time and energy.

3. Solution: Allowing them to think what they want grants you the freedom to pursue your own desires. Align your thoughts and actions with your values, and you will feel proud of yourself. When you feel proud of yourself, you won't care about anyone else's opinions.

By saying Let Them, you choose to allow people to think negative thoughts about you. When you say Let Me, you focus on the one person whose opinion truly matters—yours.

Live your wild and precious life in a way that fills you with pride.

CHAPTER 7

When Grown-Ups Throw Tantrums

Now let's explore how you have let other people's emotional reactions shape your decisions.

Adults feel emotions just like children do, and you do not have to manage someone else's reactions. When you allow other people's emotional immaturity to dictate your choices, you always come last in your own life.

I didn't realize how big of a problem this was for me, and you don't either.

You navigate guilt trips, fear disappointment, worry about someone's reaction or if "now is the right time," and tiptoe around someone's mood. You let other people's behaviors and reactions drain your energy.

It delves deeper than that. Their passive-aggressive behavior, guilt trips, and emotional outbursts influence your decisions. This explains why you agree when you truly want to decline. You give in when you should hold your ground. This explains why you struggle to set boundaries. You walk on eggshells when certain people are in a bad mood for a reason.

It may seem easier to give in to your sister's guilt trip, but you lose a crucial piece of yourself in the long run. When every interaction with your girlfriend or boyfriend drains your energy, consider this: Why do you always have to be the one who adjusts? Why do you assume the responsibility for another person's happiness — sacrificing your own in the process?

Letting other people's emotional immaturity have power over you ensures you always come last. Rather than carrying the burden of someone's disappointment, anger, or guilt, you will embrace a freeing new approach: Just Let Them react.

By saying Let Them, you allow others to experience their emotions without the pressure to fix them. When you say Let Me, you prioritize what's right for you, even if it upsets someone. This is how you take responsibility for your own life.

Stop letting someone else's guilt, anger, or disappointment manipulate you. You do not need to manage other people's emotional reactions. My therapist, Anne Davin, Ph.D., a depth psychologist and writer, taught me this. She is the smartest woman I've ever met. One day, I talked with her about creating boundaries with a particularly difficult family member.

I don't want this person to bother me. They constantly make it about themselves. You probably have someone in your family like this. An evening with this person will drain your energy. When attention shifts away from them, they find countless ways to redirect it—whether through positive or negative means.

What If We Are All Just Eight Years Old?

I talked to Anne about this person, and she said something that changed everything: "Mel, most adults are just eight-year-old children inside of big bodies."

When you're with this person and you feel triggered by something they say or how they act, imagine their fourth-grade self in the room with you.

You describe someone with the emotional maturity of an eight-year-old. Whether you like it or not, that's the reality for most adults.

As I sat there and processed what she said, it made a lot of sense. It is true. Many people struggle to process their emotions healthily and often fail to communicate their needs directly and respectfully. I definitely didn't.

Consider this: Why does your mom pout instead of expressing what's wrong? What causes your friend to give you the silent treatment? Why does your boyfriend send you texts that feel passive-aggressive when you're out with friends? Why does your sister explode and then behave as if nothing occurred an hour later?

Adults, at their core, feel emotions just like children do. They excel at concealing it... most of the time.

Here's what's beautiful about the Let Them Theory: You become more compassionate, not more judgmental. Rather than feeling frustrated, you start to realize that many people lack the tools to manage their emotions in a mature way.

No one has learned how to do this. Understand your emotions and learn how to process them in a healthy way to handle them effectively. In my experience, most people struggle to understand how to do this. I definitely didn't.

Emotional maturity requires effort and development; it doesn't come naturally or spontaneously.

This skill requires time, practice, and a strong desire to learn. My therapist is correct. Many people you encounter behave like eight-year-old children when they don't get what they want or when they experience uncomfortable emotions.

Now, with the Let Them Theory, you will learn to respond with compassion, set your boundaries, and take control of your life instead of allowing other people's emotional immaturity to dictate it.

Do the Feelings Fit the Circumstance?

At eight, feeling upset about not getting the Legos you want is a normal reaction. Your friend at school says something that hurts your feelings, and feeling sad is a natural response. If you want to watch TV and your parents say it's time for bed, feeling upset is a normal reaction.

Adult experiences hold the same truth. As an adult, getting fired often leads to feelings of frustration and demoralization, which is a normal reaction. After a breakup, you often experience a depressive state. Dr. Damour states that these reactions are all appropriate and normal emotional responses. Your mind works exactly as it should, and this serves as evidence.

As you grew up, you likely learned to suppress your feelings repeatedly. Telling a child to "get over it," "stop crying," or "calm down" trains them to suppress their feelings. People distract, avoid, or numb these normal human emotions.

Dr. Damour explained that many people experience anxiety, depression, addiction, or chronic pain because they avoid their emotions over the years, allowing them to build up inside without any outlet.

Let me say it again: You must help a child create space to process their own range of emotions. You do not need to manage another adult's emotional reactions.

Understanding this holds great significance. I will explain this in more detail.

Adult Childlike Behavior

Consider the common experience of someone in your life giving you the silent treatment. An immature adult gives the silent treatment when they feel upset and struggle to process their emotions in a healthy and respectful way.

Instead, they stop talking. They act as if nothing is wrong. They often ignore you. If you've ever received the silent treatment from a friend, family member, or co-worker, you know it's painful. Your immediate instinct drives you to figure out what you did wrong.

The person giving you the silent treatment wants your attention. A child pouting in a corner seeks a parent's comfort, just as an adult giving the silent treatment wants you to ask, "Are you okay?" "Can I do something?" and "What did I do wrong?"

The silent treatment serves as a tactic for them to avoid processing their own emotions. They aim to draw you in, hoping you'll ask what's wrong, so they can evade the responsibility of addressing it themselves.

A friend of mine did this all the time in high school. One minute we were great, and the next she stopped talking to me. I never knew what I did wrong. I tried to call her, said hello in the hallways, and sometimes begged for forgiveness for something I didn't even know I had done.

She never addressed it, and then one day she decided she was over it—and we were back to being best friends. I felt so relieved when she started talking to me again that I played along like nothing ever happened.

She found it easier to give me the silent treatment and avoid an honest conversation instead of coming to me and sharing her feelings. She had no idea how to do that.

It's important to realize that it truly has nothing to do with you.

The silent treatment comes from a person's struggle to understand their emotions or confront their past demons.

Allow them. Whenever an adult behaves like an eight-year-old child, allow it.

This strategy will change your life. A parent might get angry, storm out of the room, and refuse to talk to anybody for several days or a weekend.

In one instance, one of my best friends experienced her mother suddenly stop talking to her for a month. One day, she came down the stairs in the morning, and it felt as if nothing had ever happened.

The Let Them Theory empowers you to rise above emotional immaturity and abuse. You will know exactly how to respond.

First, you should never take on the responsibility of managing another adult's emotions. When someone gives you the silent treatment, plays the victim, or erupts in frustration, let them. Visualize an eight-year-old trapped inside their body. Doing that triggers something wild. You feel confident around this person. You truly feel sorry for them. You experience compassion rather than contempt.

Their inability to process normal human emotions like sadness, insecurity, disappointment, anger, fear, and rejection is not your fault. It's not your problem to solve. This person has experienced this since childhood.

You don't need to manage their emotions or try to fix them.

Protect yourself from their emotional spiral and see it for what it is: An individual struggles to manage or communicate their emotions healthily.

Allow them to fall silent. Allow them to erupt. Allow them to play the victim. Let them sulk. They can deny that it happened. Let them focus entirely on themselves.

Then, allow me. I will be the mature, wise, and loving adult in this situation. I will decide whether to address this directly or not at all. I need to remember that it's not my responsibility to manage someone else's emotions.

I will remove myself from any text chain, dinner table conversation, relationship, or friend group where this is happening.

Rather than waiting for others to change, take charge and change yourself. Set a higher standard for yourself and refuse to take on the responsibility of managing this emotionally immature behavior.

Leave situations where someone's ongoing emotional immaturity feels increasingly like abuse. Don't feel sorry for people who constantly play the victim. Stop making excuses for someone's obvious narcissistic behavior.

The more time you invest in a relationship with someone who behaves like an eight-year-old, the more you will feel like a parent to a child.

Recognize when you deal with someone who has a lot of internal work to do, and draw healthier boundaries around the time and energy you are willing to give them.

This person must work to build their emotional intelligence skills; otherwise, they will continue to give the silent treatment, play the victim, or act passive-aggressively. This is not a personality trait; it is a pattern.

But What If You're the Problem?

What should you do if you realize while reading this that there are times in your life when you exhibit emotional immaturity?

Your emotions overwhelm you. You are sulking. You provide the silent treatment. You express your anger through text. You portray yourself as the victim. You bark at others. You focus on yourself.

As you have this realization, here is what I want to express to you:

You are not alone. I realized that about myself too.

Seeing immature behavior in others is easy, but recognizing it in yourself requires bravery and emotional intelligence. I wasn't even eight years old. I was emotionally immature, probably at the level of a five.

I easily overwhelmed myself with emotions, throwing tantrums by venting at my husband or erupting at my kids over something trivial. I experienced times in my life when I focused solely on myself, and it damaged many friendships. Even today, when work becomes incredibly stressful, I fire off long, angry texts to my business partner expressing my frustration with everything. It's unacceptable.

I write the Let Them Theory book and apply Let Them in my life while constantly learning to create space for processing my own range of emotions. The hardest part of the Let Them Theory involves learning to feel my raw emotions without reacting immediately. It's challenging. I often find myself wanting to snap back or take control of the situation immediately. I still feel frustrated when I slip up. But that's the point: It's not about achieving perfection; it's about showing kindness to yourself and embracing growth.

I face a lifelong process, and many days, it feels like I start all over again. I recognize that this is a skill I will work on for the rest of my life, and you will too.

The Let Them Theory has played a crucial role in fostering my self-compassion. I have gained a deeper understanding of how to handle my emotions.

Applying the Let Them Theory becomes easy when another person is having a tantrum. Mastering its use to process your own emotions elevates you to rockstar status. I can confidently say that I make significantly more money, I possess greater intelligence, and I excel as a parent, spouse, and friend now that I manage my emotions effectively. I'm finally starting to feel like a mature adult.

Use the Let Them Theory to process your emotions in a healthy way: When you feel your emotions rising, embrace them. Let the anger, frustration, hurt, disappointment, sadness, grief, tears, and feelings of failure rise to the surface. Allow them.

Then, I will not react. Keep your hands away from your phone. Keep the TV off. Skip making a drink. Keep the fridge closed. And for crying out loud, don't text anyone! Notice the feelings and let them rise up.

You must learn how to Let Them rise because when they do, they also fall.

Do You Know What an Emotion Really Is?

Emotions burst as chemicals in your brain, igniting and being absorbed into your body within six seconds. Your emotional reactions occur rapidly, often remaining completely unconscious. You might first notice your emotions through the physical sensations that accompany the chemical burst, like sweating, muscle tightness, or a racing heartbeat.

Research shows that most emotions rise up and then fall away within 90 seconds if you don't react to them.

Your emotions rise up uncontrollably. Attempting to is a waste of your time. Learning to let them rise up and then fall without reacting is the better strategy. You cannot control the emotional reactions of another human being, no matter how hard you try.

Emotions spread easily. When you see someone else feeling sad, afraid, disgusted, or angry, you can feel those same emotions in your own body. This explains how someone else's tone of voice, their shift in energy, their bad mood, and their body language can immediately make you feel on edge.

One more thing to understand is that whenever you or someone else feels hungry, tired, stressed, under the influence, lonely, angry, or hurt, emotions will run higher. I notice that whenever I do or say something I later regret, stress, alcohol, or hunger usually plays a role. This knowledge empowers me to make changes that improve my emotional management and keep me in control of my words, actions, and thoughts.

One of my biggest takeaways from using the Let Them Theory is:

You cannot control what happens around you. You cannot control your emotional responses, as they occur automatically—just like your stress response activates on its own.

You can always choose how to think, speak, or act in response to others, your surroundings, or the emotions that arise within you. Your power comes from that source.

Letting other adults manage their own emotions will change your life. Learning to let your emotions rise and fall while communicating your needs, even in painful moments, is essential.

At times, making the right decision for yourself will be one of the hardest challenges you face in life.

CHAPTER 8

The Right Decision Often Feels Wrong

A listener of The Mel Robbins Podcast recently reached out to me with this question:

Mel, I got engaged and will soon marry. The wedding approaches in a few weeks, and I know this will be one of the happiest moments of my life. However, it isn't. As the wedding approaches, my fiancée and I fight more. This feeling of dread won't leave me alone. I fear I am making a huge mistake. I need to figure out what to do. My parents and hers have sent out the invitations and already put down the deposits for everything. I want to make my family proud. I want to protect my parents' money. I want to protect my fiancée's heart. I want to avoid making her parents and everyone else we know mad at me. How can I cancel this?

Reading the question, I felt my heart seize. I bet yours did as well.

When the stakes feel this high, the right answer often seems wrong.

The answer appears simple on the surface, even if it doesn't feel that way.

He should cancel it. Dreading the wedding? You're making a mistake. If you can't stop thinking about ending it, then you should do it.

The right decision may appear clear, but it isn't always easy to make. The human experience largely revolves around emotions.

What appears logical on the surface doesn't feel logical when you recognize it will inflict significant pain on others.

In life, when faced with a dilemma, you often choose to inflict pain on yourself rather than making the right decision for you, even if it will be painful for others to accept.

The groom who wrote to me understands, on an intellectual level, what he needs to do.

His emotions create the problem. He reached out to me for reassurance. He struggles to understand how to manage his feelings and how to address the emotional turmoil it will cause in others.

Struggling with a tough decision shows a mentally healthy reaction to a challenging situation. His worry about other people shows that he's a good person.

Many times in your life, people will feel mad, disappointed, or heartbroken by what you say or do. There will be.

Separate yourself from your emotions and the emotional reactions of others when determining the right decision to make.

Don't let your emotions drive your decisions; they often prevent you from making the right choices.

This proves to be much more challenging than it appears. Making the right decisions can be devastating. Being honest with someone can absolutely break your heart. That decision feels like it might destroy you from the inside out, especially when it hurts someone you love.

Consider the situation with our groom who wants to call off his wedding but struggles to find the right words. A wave of dread likely washed over you as you read the message, even though you and I don't know this person.

Emotions hold immense power.

You sense the weight in your chest as you imagine him sitting his fiancée down and saying, "We have to talk." Picture him making the phone call and telling his parents. His fiancée buries her face in her hands, and you can almost hear her sobbing. Her heart tightens as she pictures the grief clogging her throat when she calls her parents. Her dad feels the anger swelling in his chest as he experiences the heartbreak of his baby girl. "Dad, he broke it off," she might say. "The wedding was called off by him."

You read and think about the situation, and it creates an emotional reaction inside you. Letting people down and breaking their hearts stands as one of the hardest challenges you will face in life.

Adults can feel however they choose—and they can express their anger. Shattered. Heartbroken. Feeling overwhelmed. I feel embarrassed. I am extremely pissed off at you.

It's beyond your control.

You attempt to control it by avoiding the truth. Everyone has done this. You've stayed in the wrong relationships, the wrong jobs, or followed the wrong patterns of behavior for years.

You still haven't called out your friend for talking behind your back, confronted your mom, taken a leave of absence, or confessed to your best friend that you are in love with them.

Avoiding it feels easier because it allows you to escape facing it. However, making things easier now creates greater challenges later. Having the hard conversations now will lead to better outcomes next year.

From experience, I can tell you that waiting only increases the pain. When you choose not to do what's right for you, you only invite more pain into your life.

Did the groom call off the wedding? I am unsure. Do I wish he did?

Absolutely. I wish that for his sake, and I wish that for hers. Everyone deserves to be with someone who wants to be with them.

The most courageous, honorable, and kind action in life is to tell someone you don't want to be with them. Being honest proves challenging, particularly when others display emotional immaturity.

You avoid them to steer clear of their guilt, venting, and bad moods. You're not avoiding confrontation; you're avoiding someone else's emotions. The only conflict arises from your internal struggle regarding how your decisions will affect others emotionally and how they will respond.

People stay in marriages for a decade even when they know they have ended. People stay in jobs for too long because of this. People choose majors and career paths and stick with them because they fear making decisions that might affect someone else's feelings. Understanding that emotions are a normal part of life empowers you. Recognizing that adults experience ups and downs and can survive them fosters courage. You don't need to shield everyone else from experiencing emotions. Live your life in a way that aligns with your values and drives you forward.

At times, that will hurt someone. They will feel disappointed.

Your decision will cause pain or heartbreak for someone else, and facing that reality will be one of the hardest things you will do in life. I remember that when my actions might disappoint or upset someone, Dr. Damour's framing helps me see negative emotions as a mentally healthy response to life's challenges.

People feel upset when you change your mind and experience disappointment or heartbreak when you break up. People can feel depressed after losing their job.

How do you approach this, and how do you handle the intense guilt and discomfort that arise when you make a tough decision that you know is right for you?

Learn to Ride the Emotional Wave

Thinking about emotional discomfort like learning to ride a wave in the ocean has helped me. Emotions resemble waves at their core.

They ascend, they descend.

Some days, your life will feel steady, still, and calm. Some days, like the day you call off the wedding, a hurricane strikes, and you feel like you're drowning. You will not drown.

Will calling off the wedding be difficult? Absolutely. Will it become one of the most painful experiences of your life? Absolutely. Does her dad want to kill you?

Absolutely, for several months. Will your parents lose their deposit and feel angry with you? Absolutely. Will their hearts break because they also love your fiancée? Absolutely.

They will grieve the loss of what they believed could have been great.

Slowly, as you Allow them to feel whatever they need to feel, and allow yourself to feel whatever you need to feel. Don't try to control, avoid, or change it; life naturally returns to a new normal.

Your parents will eventually understand why you made the decision, and they will feel proud of your bravery in doing it.

Allow them.

Remind yourself that this too shall pass. You possess strength that surpasses any emotional reaction from others. Allow them to express their opinions. Allow them to express their reactions. Give me mine. Allow your emotions to rise and create space for yourself to process them.

Don't allow someone else's emotional reactions to stop you from making the hard decision. I will be honest with myself and others. I will tackle the hard thing that feels painful now, because it is the right choice and will spare me from much pain later. I will seize the opportunity to create the life I deserve.

Let's summarize what you learned about handling someone else's emotional reactions. You let other people's emotional reactions dictate your choices. The Let Them Theory encourages you to step back when another adult behaves immaturely.

1. Problem: You allow other people's emotional immaturity to control your life. You let someone else's outbursts, guilt trips, and reactions dictate your actions. This leads you to constantly manage their emotions instead of focusing on your own.

You always prioritize the emotional needs of others, sacrificing your own happiness.

2. Truth: You do not need to manage other people's emotional reactions. You cannot control how others feel or respond, and you cannot fix their emotional immaturity. Many adults possess the emotional capacity of an eight-year-old, and that remains unchangeable.

3. Solution: Apply the Let Them Theory to maintain control even when an adult behaves like a child and experiences an emotional outburst.

Choose the decisions that suit you best, regardless of how they affect others.

You keep your power by refusing to carry the weight of others' emotions and by acting in alignment with your values.

By saying Let Them, you allow others to experience their emotions without taking on the responsibility to manage or fix those feelings.

When you say Let Me, you embrace the courage to make the right decisions for yourself, regardless of how others may feel about them.

Now is the moment to mature and behave like an adult.

CHAPTER 9

<u>Yes, Life Isn't Fair</u>

Life isn't fair. At some point, wake up, accept that fact, and stop obsessing over what other people have, how they look, and what they've achieved.

Let's discuss something that everyone on this planet faces: Letting other people's success hold you back.

You cannot control another person's success, luck, or timing in life. You can control what you do with the examples set by others and the actions you take next.

Seeing other people's lives as proof of your failure, unattractiveness, or inadequacy makes you your biggest obstacle.

Scrolling through social media mindlessly or comparing yourself to others leaves you feeling stuck, hopeless, and always behind. You are causing yourself unnecessary pain. Other people are paralyzing you, leading to procrastination and self-criticism.

Focusing on life's unfairness and comparing yourself to others drains your motivation and hinders your progress. A self-fulfilling prophecy emerges. Your chronic habit of comparing yourself leads to your failure.

The problem lies with you. Accept the truth: Life isn't fair. It isn't.

You face an unfair burden of student debt because you couldn't afford the tuition.

Your sister looks like a supermodel, and everyone flocks to her at the bars, while you sit off to the side buying your own drinks. It's not fair.

Your supervisor keeps giving you the crappy shift at work, and that's not fair.

Your country suffers from the devastation of war.

You face the challenge of managing your insulin for your entire life due to being born diabetic.

Your friend enjoys a nice house or apartment because their parents paid for it, and that feels unfair.

Your colleague got promoted, and you didn't, which feels unfair. Getting diagnosed with breast cancer feels incredibly unfair. Your friend enjoys a seemingly perfect family life, while your own family struggles so much that they wouldn't even consider featuring you on a reality show. Your friend enjoys a fast metabolism and eats whatever she wants, which feels unfair. You face asthma because you grew up in a polluted area, and that's unfair. The rising cost of living and gas prices is unfair. Your face shouldn't break out with acne.

You are correct. It feels unfair.

Every human being receives a different hand in life, and you cannot control the cards that others hold. Spending more time staring at someone else makes you miss the entire point of the game.

In life, you play for yourself. You play with them.

Someone always has better cards than you. How you play the hand you've been dealt matters more than the hand itself.

You have been busy comparing yourself to everyone else, and you have missed one of the greatest secrets in life: Others show you how to improve your skills, and that's how you achieve victory.

Many people receive a "luckier" or "more successful" hand of cards. Allow them.

They will achieve things faster. They hold an advantage. They possess more resources. They receive more support. You cannot change it. This is a fact. Allow them.

Worrying about it or making yourself feel bad insults your intelligence. Figure out how to win. Learn how to work with what you have, start where you are, and create anything you want in life.

However, you will never achieve that if you allow this harmful habit of comparing yourself to others to take control of your power. Cease that.

Wishing everyone flocks to you instead of your sister at the bar, or that you enjoy those European vacations, or that you stand taller or have a healthier complexion, or land a better job, or receive the wedding proposal, or earn more money won't make it happen. Your confidence simply vanishes.

A world-class card player will tell you it's not about the hand you've been dealt. How you play the hand matters. To win the game of life, focus on the cards you hold and decide how to play them.

I understand! Looking at the hand you hold feels like facing the unluckiest hand on the planet. People often ask, "Why me?" Feeling sorry for yourself is easy. Looking at someone else can make you feel bad about yourself. They might have the body, the bank account, a loving relationship, perfect health, the car, the trust fund, the safety, the discipline, and the friend group. It just doesn't seem fair. Do you know what?

Life will never be fair.

Some people experience incredible luck. My friends appear to have everything figured out from the moment they were born. They seem to have gotten everything they wanted. Positive things and experiences pop up all around. They always find a way to make things work out.

Why did these people get so lucky while I didn't? Feeling sorry for yourself and getting angry at these people is easy, isn't it? Their family stands out as the best in the world; they found the love of their life in college; they exude attractiveness and showcase their talent as a gifted athlete. These people experience no setbacks. From what you can see, they appear to navigate life without the burdens of depression, anxiety, or childhood trauma that many of us face.

Comparing yourself to someone else's luck in life wastes your time.

When Comparison Is Torturing You

"But, Mel, I can't stop thinking about how much more attractive other people are, or how I wish I were taller or didn't have asthma, or wishing that my parents didn't get divorced and my family life was better."

You will inevitably compare yourself to others. People naturally look around to see what others are doing and how they measure up.

The tendency to compare isn't the problem. Your actions with the comparison are what truly matter.

Ask yourself: What do you do when you compare? Are you torturing yourself, or does it teach you something important?

People engage in two different types of comparison: torture or teacher. To use comparison to your advantage, first identify the type of comparison you are making. It's easy to tell the difference.

The first type of comparison tortures. You find yourself obsessed, caught up, or beating yourself up over something you can never change. Focusing on fixed attributes of someone else's life turns comparison into torture.

For example, natural beauty, body type, family history, height, metabolism, parents, country of origin, past experiences, and any God-given talents like athleticism, perfect pitch, genius brain power, the ability to learn languages at the blink of an eye, photographic memory, artistic talents... you understand the idea.

People often feel envious of the fixed characteristics in someone else's life, but those traits are typically innate and not the result of hard work. They received these cards, and their cards aren't going anywhere (and neither are yours).

No amount of effort on your part will make these cards appear in your life.

This is how you can tell it's fixed. Can you do something in the next 30 seconds to change this? If you don't, you won't change these things.

Understand the difference between what you can change and what you cannot. Comparing yourself to someone or some aspect of their life that you cannot change, no matter how hard you try, only tortures you.

Any time you obsess over a fixed aspect of someone else's life instead of focusing on your own, you engage in self-torture. Your growth suffers, and your happiness declines. If you can't change it, learn to allow it. Allow them.

This task proves challenging.

Our oldest daughter, Sawyer, has engaged in this first type of comparison and tortured herself for years. She hyper fixates on her younger sister, Kendall, who has a completely different body type, bone structure, metabolism, and athletic abilities. Kendall was born with an amazing singing voice and perfect pitch.

Sawyer is unable to change this. Kendall is unable to change this. I cannot change this.

Over the years, I have seen Sawyer make herself miserable and give away her power by engaging in torturous comparison. She hates her body as a result. She criticizes herself for her metabolism. She expresses frustration about the difficulty of losing weight and the ease of gaining it.

She clearly expresses her frustration about how unfair it is that Kendall can wear her clothes, while she cannot wear Kendall's.

She's right, you know. It isn't fair. No exercise, supplements, or singing lessons can change the score Sawyer keeps in her mind: Kendall wins while Sawyer loses.

Psychologists refer to this as upward comparison. Upward comparison involves measuring yourself against others whom you perceive to have better attributes than you do. Research shows it damages your self-esteem.

You seldom look around and see how much better off you are than most people in the world.

The U.N. reports that one in four people lack access to clean drinking water. If you have running water, electricity, and time to read this book, you're doing better than most people.

This reminds me of the painful comparisons and the tendency to criticize yourself for things in your life that you cannot control or change.

I feel deep sadness as I see how miserable Sawyer makes herself. I can't save her. I can't prevent her from making this kind of comparison. No amount of complimenting or reassurance will change her behavior. She must decide to change this for herself.

Until she stops torturing herself, she will never see the big, beautiful, amazing life waiting for her to embrace it. She cannot embrace the beauty of her own body. She always sees what she is not, overlooking the magnificence of what she is. She focuses on her sister and misses what the rest of us see: her unique talents, brains, and athleticism.

Stop obsessing over the cards in someone else's hands. Life does not offer fairness. Someone always has better cards than you, and comparing your hand to theirs leads to loss. Focus on your own path; that's how you win the game of life. Play with other players, not against them.

Many people develop eating disorders, face mental health issues, struggle with addiction, or experience shame due to the torturous nature of this type of comparison. I don't say this lightly because I understand it can lead to serious struggles and challenges that many people, including those I love deeply, face.

Psychologists identify the obsessive need for control as the root cause of many disorders. When you try to control something beyond your reach, you feel increasingly out of control and powerless.

Recognize when you engage in this first type of comparison.

Cease. Allow them to live their life. I will focus on mine.

Don't waste your life torturing yourself; you have too much intelligence for that. Keep your power close, as you will need it to unlock the potential of your unique life. Being happier requires you to allow yourself to be happier.

You cannot enjoy your life or love yourself while beating yourself up at the same time.

Now, let's dive into the second type of comparison. This comparison offers you a wealth of opportunities.

CHAPTER 10

How to Compare with Your Teacher

You just discovered the first type of comparison, which feels like self-torture. Now, let's discuss the second type: comparison that teaches you something. Here's how you can tell that comparison is beneficial: You examine elements of another person's life or success that you can build for yourself.

Over time and with consistent effort, you can change these aspects of your life, career, or health.

You can change countless aspects of your life: switch your job, build a better friend group, discover your purpose, spend more time with your kids, plan vacations, achieve financial freedom, wake up earlier, craft the greatest love story of your life, become an amazing cook, or get in the best shape of your life. You can buy a huge ring, a fancy watch, or a sports car; renovate your kitchen, build a second home, improve your relationship with your stepparents, develop healthier habits, write a book, heal your trauma, gain more social media followers, establish better boundaries, carve out more time for yourself, launch a business, or enhance your reputation.

I created a long list intentionally. Ninety-five percent of what you want in life is within your reach if you commit to working hard, staying consistent, being disciplined, and exercising patience. Most aspects of your life are not set in stone.

If someone has achieved something greater, larger, and more impressive than you could ever envision, allow them to shine. Allow them to achieve their success. Allow them to beat you to it. Allow them to accomplish it in the smartest and coolest way. Their success provides you with the formula. Do you recall my story about avoiding social media posts? Whatever you desire, someone else can provide the formula. Allow them to take the lead.

I didn't understand this for most of my life. When someone achieved what I wanted, I told myself they had outpaced me. I observed the people around me and viewed their successes as my failures. Seeing other people's wins as your losses makes you feel defeated before you even start.

Be careful; comparison can lead you to doubt yourself, procrastinate, and remain stuck. You can achieve the same success, but instead of working to create it, you argue against what you want. You have turned other people into a problem, and they don't need to be.

Happiness, success, and money are abundant and available for absolutely everyone, including you. It exists in limitless supply.

You are not losing anything. Happiness, success, and money await your commitment to create them. I'll say this again: No one else's wins are your losses. Change the way you look at other people's success.

More than 8 billion people inhabit this planet. When you seek evidence that someone else earns more money, sports the coolest wardrobe, enjoys the best friend group, attended a more prestigious school, maintains peak fitness, sold their company, became a New York Times bestselling author, traveled the world, or possesses anything you desire, you will discover it.

The tendency to compare isn't the problem. Using comparison to your advantage is the solution. The Let Them Theory teaches you to transform comparison from a significant problem in your life into your greatest teacher.

They've Always Been Your Teacher

I recently talked with my friend Molly. Molly excels as an interior designer. She built a successful business, employs several people, and creates beautiful work for her clients.

In our recent conversations, she consistently asks me for advice about social media, posing questions like, "Mel, how can I get myself out there?" I recognize that I must engage more on social media and enhance my marketing efforts for my business online, but I feel uncertain about where to begin.

I provided her with a straightforward list of actions she could take for her business. Post every day. Make videos that explain your projects. Share before-and-after photos. Bring on an intern to create a library of short videos for you. Enroll in a free online course to deepen your understanding of social media platforms, and choose one to concentrate on.

The steps you need to take are always very simple, just like in the example I shared earlier about building my speaking business years ago. Doing them is not the problem.

Molly called me the other day, and I immediately sensed something was off. Molly, you sound different today. Are the kids doing okay?

"Yeah, yeah, yeah," she said. The kids are doing well. I am not.

I asked, "What happened?"

She exclaimed, "I saw something the other night that sent me into a spiral." I've been freaking out ever since.

I listen and think, What the heck could have happened? Wow. This situation is very serious.

Molly has known someone in her neighborhood for a long time. Molly doesn't consider her a favorite. She's the type who constantly seeks attention and tends to irritate others. They have never clicked with each other.

This person lacks experience or a background in interior design. Now, they have entered the "design" business, started posting on social media, and their posts are blowing up. This person receives thousands of likes on her posts, and what really frustrates Molly is that everyone in the neighborhood talks about how "talented" this other woman is.

Molly vented to me, "These are just photos of her own house, and she didn't even design it!"

The night before, after a long day of work with her design clients, Molly put the kids to bed, sat down on the couch, and started scrolling.

Molly's feed was buzzing with someone special! This annoying woman.

She couldn't resist. She read every single comment and stalked the woman's website. The website appears modern and clean, while Molly's remains unchanged for three years. The other woman marketed herself impressively. She looked very professional, as if she had been doing this for years. Molly spiraled downward.

She plans to steal my clients! She will outshine me in everyone's eyes. How does she figure out how to do all this? Why didn't I do this earlier? Ugh!

She took a breath and asked, "Mel, what do you think I should do?"

I will share with you the same message I shared with my friend Molly, and I want you to keep this in mind the next time you feel overwhelmed by comparison or anger regarding someone else's actions:

You don't need anyone's pity. Feeling jealous about someone else's success? That's a positive sign. I'm thrilled for you. Your future self invites you through jealousy. It invites you to look more closely at someone else—not to make you feel inferior, but to show you what is possible.

This woman did not steal any success from Molly. She did not prevent Molly from changing her website or focusing on social media.

This woman's wins online did not equal Molly's losses. Other people will never stop you from achieving what's meant for you. They cannot. You are the only one who can prevent yourself from achieving it.

This woman reminds Molly that social media matters. The teacher leads the way. Allow them to wake you up. Allow them to achieve success. Allow them to impress you with their stunning web design.

Let Them Show That It's Possible

You might have become so immersed in your daily routine that you've overlooked what's right in front of you. You might be playing so small that you can't see the big and beautiful life ahead of you. You might be so accustomed to your usual methods that you hesitate to explore a new approach.

People demonstrate what's possible. As a teacher, when you see comparison, you realize that others aren't taking anything from you; they are giving something to you. Some people possess a beautiful ability to reveal parts of your future that you can't yet fully see.

They reveal possibilities you didn't realize existed or convinced yourself you couldn't achieve.

If someone or something is making you jealous, embrace it. Their success and wins do not diminish your chances of creating what you want. They expand it. Allow them to take the lead. Transform your jealousy into inspiration. Discover what you can achieve by following their example. The people you compare yourself to serve as mirrors, reflecting back greater possibilities—or in Molly's case, the formula and the work she avoided. I told Molly that. Allow them to take the lead.

This leads me to a crucial point: This woman has a significant reason for getting under Molly's skin. This irritating person had to be the truth. If you lack motivation in life, something painful will push you to change.

Molly watched famous interior designers for years. She talked about "doing social media" for years. She offered every excuse in the book for not making it a priority.

Until now, this irritating woman suddenly appears, lacking any prior design experience, and Molly watches her do all the things she knew she needed to do years ago.

Molly realizes that this woman from the neighborhood lacks any special advantage, talent, or resources. She's so mad because of that. This annoying woman is pushing a simple fact at Molly: If I can do it, you can do it too.

This is where comparison becomes truly fascinating. People like this in your life push you to look in the mirror and confront yourself.

Let them make you mad. Thank this person who makes you mad, because you're not really mad at them. Your anger burns inside because you're frustrated with yourself. You know you could have arrived at work sooner, and you recognize your ability to solve this problem. You simply didn't. I was in the speaking business.

This kind of comparison serves as your greatest teacher.

It doesn't just show you what you need to do; it galvanizes your power and awakens your anger. Your anger fuels your drive to move forward.

Whoever triggers you, let them. Allow them to irritate you.

Let them ignite your passion. Let them show you exactly what you want and what you need to do to get there.

Let's Talk About You

How can you transform moments of jealousy and frustration into something positive? How can you turn comparison into inspiration? Clear. Say, let me examine the data that showcases other people's successes.

Whenever you engage in the game of comparison, something truly significant occurs.

Comparison reveals the areas of your life that require more of your attention.

The time for thinking and making excuses has ended. I will get to work.

Do the work. My buddy, bestselling author Jeff Walker, always says, "Success is about putting in the reps." What does that mean?

Clear: To achieve success, lose weight, write a book, or become a YouTuber, you must show up daily and tackle the boring, irritating, and uncomfortable tasks. Put in the reps.

Consider any change you desire in your life, such as hitting the gym.

What steps do you take to build muscle? You arrive each day and you put in the work.

Famous quarterback Tom Brady recently stated about success, "The truth is you don't have to be special." Be what most people aren't: consistent, determined, and ready to put in the effort.

These people who stir up your jealousy demonstrate that while you make excuses, they put in the reps, steadily tackling the boring, hard stuff.

Tom Brady says they aren't special; they've simply been what you aren't: consistent, determined, and willing to work for it. That is the secret to my success, without a doubt.

My friend Molly comes to mind. She realized in her heart that she needed to start prioritizing this several years ago. She feels pain right now because she sees the fruits of someone else's efforts.

You will keep facing this situation until you start taking action on what you want.

Molly didn't see that beautiful website pop up overnight, and she was so mad about it. The woman worked on it for months. Molly didn't create the social media strategy by magic; it consumed her efforts. While Molly made excuses, the other woman researched, studied, learned, and created all of the posts that Molly now sees.

These people make you angry because you know you could do it too. You're just upset that you didn't start doing it much earlier. Inspiration alone won't drive you to take action.

Anger plays a crucial role. Comparison serves as one of your greatest teachers, and I bet that when it occurs, it will likely be someone you know who frustrates you. Aron is down the hall.

He suddenly quits his job and works full-time on his custom boat business that he has been building in the dark on the weekends while you have been busy going out with your friends.

You feel jealous when you see him walk out the door.

When the people you know do it, you can't make excuses for why you can't. Sitting next to Aron at work for a year reveals that there's no superpower, trust fund, or upper hand involved. They just began working on it. Now they are quitting. You feel so jealous.

That's why they had to be the ones.

Feeling upset is completely normal when you see someone's beautiful website, watch a colleague walk out the door to a new life, or step into your friend's beautiful new home. If you're serious about achieving success, maintaining your health, or reaching your goals, focus your energy wisely. Don't waste time feeling upset or jealous. Get that energy, as you have work ahead of you.

Prepare yourself for the painful moments that will occur frequently in your life. The Let Them Theory helps you recognize when comparison aims to teach you something. Jealousy opens a doorway to your future, and you must recognize when it appears, kick the door open, and walk right through it.

Letting others lead the way reveals that beneath all the fear, excuses, and wasted time lies the life you've wanted all along. Your excuses, fears, and emotions hold you back from taking control of your life right now. We've discussed these throughout this entire book.

Here, you shift from attempting to control others' thoughts, feelings, and actions. Instead, you invest your time and energy into crafting the best chapter of your life. This is so important; I will give you one more example from my life.

This story reveals that your jealousy often hides valuable lessons. In my 40s, when we struggled financially and before I built the career I have today, a friend of mine undertook a huge house renovation.

Whenever we went out to lunch or took a walk, I eagerly listened to all the details about the renovations and looked at the progress photos. Following along was so fun. Every time I left and returned to our house, I felt discouraged and sad.

The day Chris and I pulled up my friend's long, winding driveway after their renovations blew me away. My mouth dropped to the floor. The house looked beautiful.

While my friend guided us on a tour of the house, I started to spiral into comparisons. How do they have so much money?! I recall my thoughts.

I felt happy for her, but jealousy surged within me. She truly earned this, and both she and her husband worked tirelessly for years. They earned every right to build it, to talk about it, to enjoy it, and to be proud of it.

I understood this deep down, but I struggled to genuinely feel happy for my friend while battling intense jealousy and insecurity at the same time. She swung open the doors to the playroom, and I almost combusted.

"This is the upstairs play loft featuring the pool table and hangout area for the kids to enjoy now—and responsibly, when they are older, with friends," she said.

She winked at us, and we all laughed.

"Here is the bunk room where all the kiddos and their friends can have sleepovers." My kids love it so much that they refuse to sleep in their own rooms now.

I dropped my jaw. My kids always preferred going to my friend's house instead of hosting friends at ours. Are there queen-size bunk beds? A playroom sits above the garage. Hello. This was a kid's dream, and I always dreamed of having "the house" where all the kids gathered too.

At this point in the tour, I felt ready to head downstairs, grab a bottle of wine, and crawl into one of these queen-size bunk beds—that's how sorry I felt for myself. I felt like a horrible person for allowing my jealousy to sour my true happiness for her. She is an incredible friend, loved by everyone, and gorgeous inside and out. Now, she has my dream home.

I tried to push the pit in my stomach down as the night went on. I acted as if I was completely unbothered by it all. Once I got in the car with Chris and we headed home, I let the jealousy out. I threw it at him.

I threw a full-blown tantrum in front of him, just like any typical eight-year-old would.

"I'll never have a house like that," I snapped. "What made you choose the restaurant business?"

Chris sat in silence, unsure of what to say, as we drove home.

This story comes to life with detail because we have unpacked this moment in marriage counseling countless times. This story centers on a house. No, it wasn't. I needed to discover a much deeper truth. I compared myself to my friend, and the anger I felt taught me a life-changing lesson.

I didn't feel mad at her. I wasn't mad at my husband at all. I felt mad at myself for giving up on my own ambition. I counted on my husband to succeed and provide me with the financial support to have the things I wanted in life. Your life is your responsibility. To achieve financial success, you must take responsibility for creating it. To get a house with queen bunk beds and a renovated kitchen, you must work for it.

I avoided that responsibility for a decade. This experience made me confront myself and recognize what I truly wanted. My future self sent me a message through jealousy. Watching my friend win opened my eyes to greater possibilities for my own victory.

I kicked the door open and got to work. I am just like everyone else. I just did what I previously avoided. I remained consistent, determined, and ready to work for what I wanted. I began putting in the reps. I worked hard for 15 years to get my queen-size bunk beds. I did it, and you can too.

The Let Them Theory helps you dig deep and uncover the truth about what jealousy teaches you and where you have let yourself down. When you stay on the surface, wasting your time and energy on others and things beyond your control, you miss out on discovering the deeper meaning and possibilities in your life.

Live your beautiful and amazing life to the fullest. Your potential exceeds your imagination. Your location, current circumstances, and perceived limitations do not define you.

Be honest with yourself about what you truly want and take responsibility for creating it; you will achieve it. You're not required to be special. Get up every day, put one foot in front of the other, and work hard to improve a little bit each day, striving to be better than you were yesterday. One day, you will wake up and see that you have changed yourself and are now living the life you once envied.

Let's summarize what you learned about overcoming chronic comparison. You have let other people's success paralyze you until now. The Let Them Theory encourages you to embrace others' successes and use that inspiration to create the life you desire.

1. Problem: Focusing on life's unfairness and comparing yourself to others wastes your precious time and energy on things beyond your control. You allow others' success to paralyze you, which keeps you stuck and feeling behind and frustrated. This mindset drives procrastination and perfectionism, stopping you from taking action to create your own success.

2. Truth: Someone will always be luckier, possess what you desire, progress further, or achieve success faster than you.

Comparing yourself to others happens naturally, but when it takes over your thoughts, it weakens your confidence and motivation. You cannot control the success of others, but you can control your response to it.

3. Solution: Embrace the Let Them Theory. Stop torturing yourself and leverage comparison to your advantage. Embrace the success of others and use it to drive your own journey forward. Success achieved by others shows that you can achieve it as well. Turn inspiration into action, and you start building the extraordinary life you deserve.

When you say Let Them, you learn from other people's success and allow them to lead the way. When you say Let Me, you focus on playing the cards in your hand, turning inspiration into action, and winning by collaborating with others, not competing against them.

CONCLUSION

Your Let Me Era Is Here

We have spent a lot of this book discussing others: their opinions, their emotions, and how their actions annoy, anger, frustrate, or disappoint you. This book focuses on the individual experience. You matter.

If you believe it's about them, you've missed the point. Think other people are the problem? Go back and read this entire book again. The truth is clear: YOU possess the power. You are the one giving it away.

Picture yourself beneath a sky that shifts constantly—sometimes clear and blue, other times filled with clouds, or rumbling with storms.

You spend so much time and energy trying to keep that sky clear, wishing away the clouds and hoping for endless sunshine. The sky ignores your desires. It does what it does, with or without your input.

You reach a breakthrough moment when you realize this: The sky's beauty remains intact despite the presence of clouds or storms. The variety and unpredictability make it truly magnificent. The storms emphasize the calm; the clouds enhance the value of the sun. Your life reflects the same truth.

You try to control the uncontrollable, forcing the world to conform to your expectations. What if you focused on your own response to whatever the world throws your way? Changing the weather isn't possible. You can change how it impacts you.

You control how everything around you impacts your life.

A comment from a loved one can either destroy your self-esteem or roll off your back, and you get to choose how it affects you. You determine whether the bad dates you've experienced lead you to lower your standards or to become even more discerning. You choose whether someone else's success drives you to quit or motivates you to put in even more effort.

It's simple. Embrace your power.

This realization feels like finally grasping the true nature of the sky.

You now see the clouds that once frustrated you as part of a larger, ever-changing masterpiece. The storms that once frightened you now showcase power and beauty, teaching you resilience and strength. You begin to recognize that the sky's unpredictability creates its magnificence and endless fascination.

Consider that for a moment. The sky acts as it will—clouds gather, storms arrive, and the sun shines when it chooses. You can't control it, but you can control your navigation beneath it. Carry an umbrella, dance in the rain, and chase the sun when you need to.

The people and situations around you change like the weather. You can never control other people—their thoughts, their actions, their feelings for you, or how quickly they notice you at the grocery store.

Why would you ever give them that level of control over you?

Why would you entrust something as precious as your confidence, your peace of mind, your happiness, and your dreams to the whims and moods of those around you?

Not using Let Them means you let the worries, actions, insecurities, and opinions of others affect you. If you don't use Let Me, you leave the things you want in life to chance.

Take a moment to truly reflect and ask yourself: Imagine channeling all the energy and time you spend resisting reality—wishing lines would move faster, hoping for quicker replies, seeking recognition from your boss, desiring more friends, craving approval from others, longing for family support in your career change—into something that truly matters to you. Where would you be? Who will you become? What did you achieve?

The cost of not using Let Them is significant.

Consider all the missed opportunities—the people you wanted to introduce yourself to, the career you aimed to pursue, the music, the stand-up, the book you never wrote, the photo you didn't post, the trip you didn't book, the thing you hesitated to say, the person you hesitated to love.

The cost of not using Let Me is significant.

Can you truly pay that price? I realize I cannot.

We often create excuses to justify why those who possess what we desire are different from us: They were born into wealth. They look more attractive. They find life easier. They got lucky.

I'm sorry to say this, but that's just an excuse. You are just like the people you see achieving extraordinary things. They lack uniqueness.

One thing is clear: They refuse to let the world around them derail their dreams. They navigate the sky, accept the weather as it comes, and keep moving toward their goals no matter what. Eventually, they grew weary of worrying about others' opinions and took charge, diving into their work.

They wake up every day with laser focus, proving through their actions that they are worthy and deserving of the vision they hold for their life.

Each day you let your fear of someone else's opinion, stress over friendships, or worry about reactions stop you from making the phone call, filling out the application, working on the business plan, starting the diet, or putting in the effort, you hold yourself back. You are limiting your own potential. Life moves on around you while you stand still.

Focus on what truly matters and let go of the countless insignificant details.

Use every second of your day for all the amazing things you know you can achieve.

Don't allow the fear of others' opinions to hold you back. Now is the moment to pursue your dreams with boldness, relentless energy, and no apologies.

Take charge and express yourself without worrying about others' feelings. Now is the moment to fiercely guard your own peace.

Don't allow the success of others to bring you down. Now is the moment to start working.

Take charge of your social life instead of relying on others. Now is the moment to create the most incredible friendships you've ever experienced.

Stop attempting to change those who resist change. Let adults be adults.

Stop rescuing those who struggle. Now is the moment to allow others to heal in their own way.

Quit wasting your time trying to make people love you. Choose the love you deserve now.

Now is the moment to take back your power and take back your life.

The Let Them Theory empowers you to reclaim your power.

Live the life you've always wanted. Become a millionaire.

Experience the beautiful love story you've always dreamed of. Build a career that challenges and fulfills you.

Will YOU allow yourself to do it?

No one else can stop you. You have the responsibility.

Understanding that you are responsible for your own happiness stands as the most important part of the Let Them Theory. You hold the power to influence the energy you bring and the way you present yourself. Wake up every day and put in the effort to make progress on what matters. You define what matters to you. You must tell the truth, even when it's really hard. You must pay for your life. You don't owe anyone anything, but you owe yourself everything.

If you're not where you want to be, take responsibility; it's all on you.

The great news is, once you decide, you can change it.

You've spent too many years focusing on other people, their feelings, their thoughts, and their actions. This book serves as your wake-up call: You take charge.

This realization frees us; it does not condemn us.

It's incredible to realize that others can't affect you. Isn't it liberating to realize that they can say and do whatever they choose—they can mock, question, achieve great success, and you stay unbothered?

How amazing is it that YOU control what you think, what you say, and what you do?

Isn't it incredible that YOU decide where to invest your time and energy, and what you accept or decline?

Reclaim your power by taking responsibility for your life. Demand more of yourself because time is ticking, and you've wasted enough of it worrying about things that don't matter. Focus on what you can control and ignore everything else.

Consider the sky again. You will decide how to navigate whatever it brings and however it changes. You choose how to respond, how to act, and how to live. The clouds, the storms, and the sunshine all have their place, but they do not define you. You shape your identity.

I won't lie to you: It will be challenging. Starting to say Let Them doesn't mean you instantly get everything you've ever wanted. Anyone who makes that promise is lying to you.

The moment you reclaim your power, you can find comfort in knowing that it's only a matter of time. You control your career, your partner, your friends, your body, and your goals.

Now that we're here, I feel an incredible excitement to personally welcome you to your Let Me era.

I will get started.

I will take a risk.

I will write the book.

I want to be honest about my desires.

I will get in the best shape of my life.

I will apply for the dream job.

I will stop giving love to people who don't want me back.

I will create a better life. I live a life that fills me with pride. I live a life that brings me happiness. I will use my precious energy to enjoy every single moment of my life.

This book reveals that you have always held control. You have always taken charge. You always hold the power. It's time to reclaim it.

I want you to understand that no matter how crazy, unlikely, or silly that big dream you envision for yourself may appear, I believe in it for you. If you don't believe in yourself, let me believe in you. If you're unsure whether you can do it, let me show you how.

If you don't know where to start, I can help you take the first step.

I want to make sure you know: I love you, I believe in you, and I trust you to unlock all the magic and joy that your amazing life offers.

Two simple words are all it takes:

Allow me.

www.ingramcontent.com/pod-product-compliance
Lightning Source LLC
Chambersburg PA
CBHW072143130225
21937CB00007B/303